GENDER
AND ECONOMIC
DEVELOPMENT

United Nations Human Settlements Programme
Nairobi 2011

UN@HABITAT

The Global Urban Economic Dialogue Series
Gender and Economic Development

First published in Nairobi in 2011 by UN-HABITAT.
Copyright © United Nations Human Settlements Programme 2011

All rights reserved
United Nations Human Settlements Programme (UN-HABITAT)
P. O. Box 30030, 00100 Nairobi GPO KENYA
Tel: 254-020-7623120 (Central Office)
www.unhabitat.org

HS/033/11E
ISBN(Series): 978-92-1-132027-5
ISBN(Volume): 978-92-1-132335-1

Disclaimer

Cover photo © World Bank

Acknowledgements:

Director:	Oyebanji Oyeyinka
Chief Editor and Manager:	Xing Quan Zhang
Principal Author:	Elissa Braustein
English Editor:	Eric Orina
Design and Layout:	Andrew Ondoo
Suppport:	Lucia Kiwala, Everngelista Mutandi
Printing:	UNON, Publishing Services Section, Nairobi, ISO 14001:2004-certifie

FOREWORD

Urbanization is one of the most powerful, irreversible forces in the world. It is estimated that 93 percent of the future urban population growth will occur in the cities of Asia and Africa, and to a lesser extent, Latin America and the Caribbean.

We live in a new urban era with most of humanity now living in towns and cities.

Global poverty is moving into cities, mostly in developing countries, in a process we call the *urbanisation of poverty*.

The world's slums are growing and growing as are the global urban populations. Indeed, this is one of the greatest challenges we face in the new millennium.

The persistent problems of poverty and slums are in large part due to weak urban economies. Urban economic development is fundamental to UN-HABITAT's mandate. Cities act as engines of national economic development. Strong urban economies are essential for poverty reduction and the provision of adequate housing, infrastructure, education, health, safety, and basic services.

The Global Urban Economic Dialogue series presented here is a platform for all sectors of the society to address urban economic development and particularly its contribution to addressing housing issues. This work carries many new ideas, solutions and innovative best practices from some of the world's leading urban thinkers and practitioners from international organisations, national governments, local authorities, the private sector, and civil society.

This series also gives us an interesting insight and deeper understanding of the wide range of urban economic development and human settlements development issues. It will serve UN member States well in their quest for better policies and strategies to address increasing global challenges in these areas

Joan Clos
Under-Secretary-General, United Nations
Executive Director, UN-HABITAT

TABLE OF CONTENTS

ABBREVIATIONS

DAW	United Nations Division for the Advancement of Women
E	Exit
ECLAC	Economic Commission for Latin America and the Caribbean
FAO	Food and Agriculture Organization of the United Nations
G	Level of Globalization
GAD	Gender and Development
GDI	Gender Development Index
GDP	Gross Domestic Product
GEI	Social Watch Gender Equity Index
GEM	Gender Empowerment Measure
GEP	Gender-specific Environmental Parameter
GGG	Global Gender Gap Index
HDI	Human Development Index
HIPC	Heavily Indebted Poor Countries
HIV/AIDS	Human Immunodeficiency Virus/Acquired Immunodeficiency Syndrome
IMF	International Monetary Fund
ILO	International Labour Organization
K	Physical Capital
L	Labor
MDG	Millennium Development Goal
MDG3	Millennium Development Goal 3
MENA	Middle East and North Africa
OECD	Organisation for Economic Cooperation and Development
P	Population
PC	Provisioning Capacity
UN	United Nations
UNDESA	United Nations Department of Economic and Social Affairs
UNDP	United Nations Development Programme
UNECA	United Nations Economic commission for Africa
UNIFEM	United Nations Development Fund for Women
UNRISD	United Nations Research Institute for Social Development
SAP	Structural Adjustment Program
SIGE	Standardized Index of Gender Equality
SNA	System of National Accounts
WAD	Women and Development
WEF	World Economic Forum
WID	Women in Development
WTO	World Trade Organisation

LIST OF FIGURES AND TABLES

TABLES

FIGURES

CHAPTER 1   **INTRODUCTORY OVERVIEW**

This report reviews research and policy in the field of gender and economic development, with particular emphasis on economic literature and practice. "Gender" is a social construct, and refers to the social meaning of and expectations assigned to being biologically male or female, the relationships between women and men, and the nature of the social and economic hierarchies that these relationships produce. Gender as meaning, expectations, relationships and hierarchies vary by nation, race/ethnicity, class, stage of the life cycle, level of economic development and structure of production. In the context of economic development, we will use the term gender to refer to how sex structures the division of work, rights, responsibilities, and resources, and how these divisions are in turn reflected in economic institutions and dynamics.

The first two sections provide context for the remainder of the report. The first section begins with a short history of gender and economic development thought, tracing the transition from women in development in the 1970s to the gender and development approach that dominates development thought today. It then contrasts how gender and development has been applied at the World Bank versus the UN as an example of the range of institutional approaches to gender and development, and discusses the outcomes of recent efforts to mainstream gender in development institutions more generally. The second section provides a statistical overview of women and men in developing countries, covering data on employment, the Millennium Development Goals, and composite indices of gender equality.

The fourth section sets out an analytical framework for applying gender and economic development concepts to policy by outlining models of production relations in the household and the macroeconomy. In the household model we emphasize how gender structures the conditions of provisioning, and the consequences for women's empowerment and human capabilities. We contrast standard economic approaches to the macroeconomy with one that reflects how meso-level institutions like markets or the public sector are themselves "bearers of gender," explicitly incorporating the production of human capabilities in the domestic sector.

The final four sections survey a sample of current gender and economic development issues, using the analytical framework developed in the prior section to both evaluate current practices and policies and to consider how gender and development concepts can be used to improve upon them. We emphasize the macroeconomic aspects of gender and economic development, though the microeconomic constraints and conditions drawn out in the household model are continually referenced to measure empowerment and well-being. Both directions of micro-meso-macro pathways are covered. Section 5 on globalization, liberalization and women's empowerment and section 6 on the gendered terrain of central bank policy focus on the effects of macroeconomic conditions and policy on women and communities, while section 7 on gender inequality and economic growth and section 8 on the macroeconomics of development and care discuss how gender relations at the micro- and meso-levels affect the aggregate economy. Section 9 concludes.

CHAPTER 2 A HISTORY OF GENDER AND ECONOMIC DEVELOPMENT THOUGHT AND POLICY APPROACHES

2.1 From Women in Development to Gender and Development

In this section, we give a brief overview of how the theory and practice of gender and economic development have evolved since the 1970s. Most reviews of this type begin by identifying three distinctive schools of thought: women in development, women and development, and finally gender and development. Each of these approaches is based on different understandings of and assumptions about the development process, the role of women and men in this process, and thus how to conduct policy in relation to these linkages. Though they are roughly chronological in their genesis, from women in development to women and development to gender and development, there is overlap among them, as well as contemporaneous versions in research and policy today. Table 1 gives a summary outline of the three approaches, indicating their origins, key arguments, implications for public policy, and a list of some of the main criticisms that have been directed at each. (Note that some of the critiques of women in development and gender and development will be discussed more at length in the next two sections on mainstreaming gender.)

The place to begin is with the wider stage of development thought, as it is here that the notions of "women" and "gender" as distinctive and important categories for development were either: (1) conspicuously missing, or (2) identified as simply inaccurate and potentially damaging to women themselves and the development process generally. Development thought in the 1950s and 1960s was dominated by modernization theory – the belief that all developing countries would pass through a set of pre-determined and identical stages of economic growth and development propelled largely by physical capital accumulation (Todaro and Smith 2006). According to this view, development would bring with it the benefits of industrialization: higher living standards, wages and education levels, and better health (Rathgeber 1990). With the emphasis on capital accumulation in the context of aggregate models of growth, early development research and practice predictably gave little to no consideration to women as a distinctive group (Ibid.).

This is the context in which economist Ester Boserup published her now famous book *Woman's Role in Economic Development* in 1970. Up to that point, development theory was an almost exclusively male enterprise (Elson 1999), and it was the first time that an economist claimed that economic development treated women differently from men (Benería 2001a). Boserup argued that women had been marginalized in the modernization process, and that extant practices of growth, development, and development policy threatened to actually make women worse off (Ibid: xi).

Influenced by Boserup's work, a network of Washington, D.C.-based female development professionals originated the term "women in development" (WID) in the early 1970s (Moser 1993). These and other early WID advocates promoted policies and programs that drew women into modernization, for example by increasing female labor force participation in industrializing sectors via targeted education and training (Benería

TABLE 1: A Taxonomy of Approaches to Women and Economic Development Thought

	Origins	Key Arguments	Policy Implications	Critiques
Women in Development	Early 1970s: Critiques of industrialization as leaving women out of modern economic development 1980s: Incorporates neoclassical/free market arguments	Integrating women into development is economically efficient, contributing to both growth and development	Promote women's economic participation by creating the conditions for markets to work Key areas for intervention include education, changing formal rules, and countering cultural stereotypes	Over-reliance on the market mechanism as a solution to women's development problems Women treated merely as a conduit for development and economic growth Does not fundamentally challenge gender stereotypes, especially as regards the traditional sexual division of labor Tends to focus on women in isolation of the social, economic and political institutions that marginalize them
Women and Development	Late 1970s: Marxist/Socialist and Third World critiques of capitalist development and modernization theory	Women are not marginalized from development, but rather integrated on unequal terms that reflect and sustain hierarchical relations between the First and Third Worlds	Promotion of income-generating projects for women that are locally-oriented Industrial development, inclusive of women, that is sheltered from global economic volatility	Overly focused on the international relations of production Tends to leave out the reproductive sector in analysis and policy Excludes consideration of intra-class or intra-ethnic relations between women and men
Gender and Development	Early 1980s: Combining work on gender from psychology, sociology and critical studies with Women and Development critiques of capitalist development paradigm	Women's economic (and a number of general development) problems based on gender – the social relations of production and reproduction between women and men. Prevailing social, political and economic models and institutions must be critically evaluated and challenged to effect transformative changes.	Advocacy of women's empowerment as a goal in and of itself Focus on equality and social justice rather than economic growth Inclusion of men in policies and programs Mainstream gender into all aspects of development policy	Development institutions have widely adopted the language of gender, but there is little policy change In turning to gender, risks diversion of development funding away from women-specific issues Emphasis of differences among women by class or ethnicity obscures their commonalities as women No strategy for the institutional transformation necessary to effect real change

2001a). WID proponents also adopted an explicit equality argument, particularly as it applied to enabling women to participate equally in modern production (Kabeer 1994). In keeping with the goals of modernization theory and policy, the WID approach rationalized equality between women and men on efficiency grounds, arguing that women were an untapped resource whose inclusion in the modern economy would ultimately benefit growth and development (Moser 1993).

These arguments for equality were cast on a shifting stage of development thought and practice, however. By the 1970s development researchers and practitioners were turning towards frameworks and policies that more directly addressed poverty and basic needs, partly because of the failure of modernization approaches to deliver significant improvements in the welfare of the world's poor (Elson 1997). This new welfare-oriented approach to development incorporated WID insights by acknowledging that women's roles were different from men's in ways important to development and policy effectiveness. The basic needs framework of the 1970s tended to subordinate and stereotype women's roles, however; development institutions treated women primarily as housewives and mothers, and men as household heads and productive agents (Kabeer 1994). The result was that men maintained their positions as the main targets of development policy, with women becoming passive recipients of welfare assistance or merely conduits to fulfilling their families' basic needs (Kabeer 1994; Rathberger 1990). Kabeer (1994) further argues that the (largely male-staffed) development agencies of the time saw WID's early equality principle as too extreme in terms of the political and economic costs that the required redistribution and equal opportunity measures would entail. So it was not just the shift from modernization theory to welfare and basic needs in development thought that stalled WID calls for equality, it was also the difficulty of effecting

institutional and social change. Granted, the welfarist approaches of the 1970s did include development projects for women's income generation, but "women's problems [were defined] in terms of the family's basic needs rather than their unequal access to income" and did little to fundamentally challenge unequal social and economic relations between women and men (Kabeer 1994: 7).

Modernization theory also met with mounting criticism from developing country intellectuals and Marxists in the 1970s, giving rise to a variety of dependency-oriented schools of thought that argued that existing structures of international inequality served to maintain the advantage of the developed world (Todaro and Smith 2006). Drawing from these dependency theories as well as explicitly Marxist and socialist critiques of capitalist development, women and development (WAD) proponents critiqued Boserup and WID as ignoring how women's economic marginalization was linked to the development model itself (Benería 2001a). The problem was not that women were marginalized from development, but rather the unequal terms under which they were incorporated (Elson 1999). Women have always been a part of the development process, according to WAD, but in a manner that supports existing structures of inequality internationally (Ratheberger 1990). In two classic articles detailing the WAD perspective, Benería and Sen (1981, 1982) argued that the key concept should be subordination in the context of new capitalist forms of insecure and hierarchical job structures, not marginalization as WID approaches emphasized.

Wider political, economic and intellectual events soon reshaped these discussions as economic stagnation and crises in both the developed and developing worlds created the conditions for a "neoclassical counterrevolution" in economic theory and policy in the late 1970s and early 1980s. Based on a fundamental belief in the supremacy of free markets, small and non-interventionist government, and free global flows of trade and finance, the neoclassical approach constituted a stark departure from the post-World War II Keynesian confidence in activist economic policies. The new neoclassical terrain of the 1980s affected development in a couple of ways: development economics became dominated by neoclassical economists who saw the major obstacles to development as policy-induced price distortions and imperfect markets, and the twin goals of liberalization and privatization replaced traditional development planning (Elson 1999). The WID efficiency argument for equality dovetailed nicely with neoclassical economic theory. Discrimination against women in labor, credit and land markets were cast as market imperfections; gender inequalities in health and education as inefficient obstacles to enabling women to live up to their full economic potential. The neoclassical counterrevolution solidified WID's efficiency argument for equality between women and men, an emphasis that continues into today.

It was in this context that the notion of "gender" – the socially constructed roles of women and men that dictate how sex determines one's role in production and reproduction – made its way into development thought (Benería 2001a). Many critics of WID argued that it failed to sufficiently address the differential power relations between women and men, and tended to over-emphasize women's productive (as opposed to reproductive) roles (Kabeer 1994; Rathgeber 1990; Razavi and Miller 1995). True, early welfare-based development programs at times provided assistance like help with hygiene or childcare, but these mostly assumed that just giving women another income-generating activity would be sufficient to alleviate women's reproductive constraints (Rathgeber 1990). Furthermore, WID implicitly presumed that women's marginalization from the development process was largely the result of cultural bias and stereotypes, so

better data, education and formal rules for equality were put forth as key to transforming these processes in development planning (Kabeer 1994). Indeed, in keeping with the neoclassical perspective, discrimination against women could be viewed as more of a market imperfection than the intentional exercise of power. Since women and men are rational economic actors, planners need only get the prices/rules/information right to bring about equality *and* economic efficiency.

By contrast, drawing from insights developed in psychology, sociology, and critical studies, gender and development (GAD) theorists shifted from understanding women's problems as based on their sex (i.e. their biological differences from men) to understanding them as based on gender – the social relations between women and men, their social construction, and how women have been systematically subordinated in this relationship (Moser 1993). At their most fundamental, GAD perspectives link the social relations of production with the social relations of reproduction – exploring why and how women and men are assigned to different roles and responsibilities in society, how these dynamics are reflected in social, economic, and political theories and institutions, and how these relationships affect development policy effectiveness. Women are cast not as passive recipients of development aid, but rather active agents of change whose empowerment should be a central goal of development policy (Grown 2008a; Moser 1993; Rathgeber 1990). One could argue that GAD grew out of WAD, combining a gender perspective and a concern for equality and social justice with a critical approach to the confidence in free market solutions proffered by neoclassical theory. In direct contrast to WID, GAD theorists aimed for social transformation, both in terms of the relations between women and men, and the definition and goals of the development model itself (Grown 2008a; Jackson and Pearson 1998; Moser 1993).

An early example of the GAD approach is the gender and structural adjustment literature, which critiqued economic models of adjustment as having unintended consequences because of being gender-blind (Collier 1994; Elson 1991; Palmer 1992). In implementing the economic management techniques dictated by neoclassical economic theory, international financial institutions like the World Bank and the International Monetary Fund responded to low growth and balance of payments crises in the developing world in the 1980s with a policy agenda that included liberalization, privatization, and a shift of labor from nontradable to tradable sectors (Elson 1999). Elson (1991) argued that the economic models underlying SAP logic, by completely ignoring the reproductive sector, essentially treated all labor as a non-produced means of production and assumed unlimited supplies of female labor. These models implicitly presumed that women would maintain their traditional roles of providing care in the household and community regardless of external economic conditions, thereby making up for the SAP-induced cuts in public spending, increases in the costs of living, and general and severe bouts of economic contraction. The unintended consequence was a type of social dislocation and disinvestment in human beings that ultimately detracted from the economic goals of the SAPs themselves, Elson and others argued.

2.2 Gender and Development in the Institutional Mainstream

The changes in development thought that have characterized the modern era – from the people-centered development approaches of the 1990s to the Millennium Development Goals in the 2000s – were accompanied by an incorporation of GAD insights into the institutional mainstream, with all sorts of development institutions adopting the language of gender and ostensibly promoting women's empowerment. But both WID's efficiency-based instrumentalism (i.e. that gender equality should be promoted because it is good for growth and development), and its tendency to focus on women in isolation rather than the gendered components of social and economic transformation more holistically, are still salient features of women and economic development thought and policy today. Part of this is probably due to what Razavi and Miller call WID's "strategy of relevance": conforming to the demands of challenging established institutional dynamics and making gender equality a key part of the development dialogue (Razavi and Miller 1995:2). Another persistent feature that is associated with WID is the extent of confidence in market-based solutions and the soundness of neoclassical theory. A good way to view these overlaps and contradictions is by exploring how they manifest in two diverse international development institutions, the World Bank and UN, and how efforts to incorporate gender concerns in the international development community more generally via "mainstreaming" have fared.

The World Bank's official position on gender and economic development is squarely in the efficiency argument camp (e.g. World Bank 2001; 2006). "Gender equality is smart economics," as the World Bank's current Gender Action Plan is titled, is a clear expression of this view (World Bank 2006). That said, the notion of "engendering development" at the World Bank is more extensive than simply using gender equality to raise rates of economic growth. The Bank defines gender equality in the context of development in terms of rights (legal equality), resources (equality of opportunity), and voice (equality in the ability to shape and contribute to the development process) (World Bank 2001). This definition is reminiscent of some early WID concerns, such as legal equality and ensuring women's access to the modern sector. While gender equality is lauded as important in its own right, there is repeated (and practical?)

emphasis on the contributions that it will ultimately make to growth and development. And as tends to be the case when emphasizing economic efficiency, World Bank approaches regularly espouse an unwavering confidence in the market mechanism to promote gender equality.

Equality of opportunity, a cornerstone of the World Bank's wider approach to equity and development, refers to economist John Roemer's theory of equal opportunity. The basic philosophical idea is that social welfare cannot be maximized if individual outcomes differ because of differences in individual circumstances (i.e. factors that individuals do not control, like how much their parents invest in their education). By contrast, inequalities that result from different levels of effort or individual choice should not be a moral or an economic concern (Roemer 2006). For gender inequality in opportunities, examples of gender-determined differences in individual circumstances are many, ranging from the gender-based wage gap to gender-based violence to nutritional gender bias (Buvinic and Morrison 2008).In a fascinating review of the World Bank's 2006 *World Development Report: Equity and Development*, Roemer criticizes the Bank for going too far in casting equity as a means to development: "[To] claim improving equity is the *best way* to maximize 'prosperity' or GDP per capita is surely *false*. The easiest way to see this is to note that, except in singular situations, one cannot simultaneously maximize two objective functions" (Roemer 2006: 238). The same can surely be said about the efficiency argument for gender equality.

By contrast, the UN and its many development-oriented agencies, have been more friendly to heterodox (non-neoclassical) approaches to economics and development, as well as GAD practitioners more concerned with targeting women's well-being and empowerment than economic growth per se. This stance is in line with the UN's adoption

of Amartya Sen's capability approach to human development as the centerpiece of its development philosophy. Capabilities refer to "what people can or cannot do, e.g. whether they can live long, escape avoidable morbidity, be well nourished, be able to read and write and communicate, take part in literary and scientific pursuits, and so forth" (Sen 1984: 497). Sen argued that the focus cannot be on just commodities (or, by extension, economic growth), because the conversion of commodities into human capabilities differs along a number of parameters such as sex, health, and class background (Ibid: 511).

In 1995, the same year as the UN's Fourth World Conference on Women in Beijing, the *Human Development Report* (published annually by the UNDP since 1990) was devoted to the issue of gender equality. In line with the human development focus on enlarging people's choices, the notion of gender equality advocated in this early report, and reflected in much of the UN's work on gender since, combines advocating for equality of rights and opportunities between women and men with treating women as agents of change. Enhancing women's capabilities and empowerment is valued both as an end in and of itself, and as a means to enhance development and growth: "Human development, if not engendered, is endangered" (UN 1995: 14). While not as closely anchored to an efficiency argument as the WID or World Bank approaches to gender and economic development, the UN's capability approach to gender equality is explicitly cognizant of the complementarities between human capabilities and more standard notions of development as economic growth and industrialization. But there is some danger here of diluting the human development message. Diane Elson notes that international aid agencies have taken the notion of human development primarily as a push to focus on investing in human as well as physical capital, so labor is still viewed primarily as a factor of production rather than as an aspect of the ultimate target of development, human capacity (Elson 1999: 105). In terms of gender, one can see how this tendency could transform policy statements on the importance of women's capabilities and empowerment to policy implementations that merely invest in women for the sake of raising incomes or rates of economic growth.

2.3 Mainstreaming Gender

Addressing this possibility, and keeping the goal of gender equality squarely at the center of institutional development work, for both the UN and other international agencies, is what drove the adoption of the principle of "gender mainstreaming" in the 1995 Beijing Platform for Action (Grown 2008a). Gender mainstreaming is a strategy for institutional transformation, one that seeks to firmly embed the goals of gender equality and women's empowerment in all aspects of development analysis, planning, and implementation. It has three elements: (1) Assessment of the implications for women and men of any legislation, policy or program; (2) Institutionalizing gender concerns in organizations themselves, for instance through staffing or organizational culture; and (3) Empowering women to ensure that they have a voice in agenda setting and policy decisions (Moser and Moser 2005; UN 1997).

Since its adoption, gender mainstreaming has become a near universal practice among international development agencies, at least in terms of adopting the terminology of gender equality and gender mainstreaming. But evaluations of gender mainstreaming have been universally critical of the apparent disconnect between having an official policy and following through via actual interventions (Grown 2008a; Moser and Moser 2005; Standing 2007). Some identify this as an institutional problem, arguing that there is no analysis of complex institutional dynamics in gender mainstreaming. For instance, development

institutions are largely male-dominated and the organizational culture often male-biased, so mainstreaming sometimes meets with resistance among staff, from senior management to field staff (Moser and Moser 2005). There is little accountability, monitoring, and evaluation, and responsibility for gender mainstreaming is often vested in the commitment and skills of just a few individuals in the organization (Ibid.). Others are not surprised at these problems, as implementing gender equality is a fundamentally political process aimed at social transformation, somewhat far afield from the largely technical process of gender mainstreaming in the context of a bureaucracy (Grown 2008a).

Certainly part of the problem is the relative absence of men in GAD work, both as practitioners and targets of analysis. Even though GAD's focus on gender relations, rather than women alone, is more inclusive of men, incorporating men presents both practical difficulties (of the sort that plagues gender mainstreaming), and political anxiety over shifting any focus away from women to include men (Chant 2000). But excluding men is ultimately detrimental for women and the promise of GAD, not least because women are tasked as the sole agents of social change, a heavy burden that would certainly be lightened if men are actively and intentionally engaged in changing gender relations as well. Examples of efforts like these are multiplying within both the UN system and the NGO community, as changing gender relations around issues like the distribution of care responsibilities or stopping violence against women must clearly involve men to be successful.[1]

---

1 See, for instance, the discussion and background papers for the Fifty-third Session of the Commission on the Status of Women, which focused on the Equal Sharing of Responsibilities between Women and Men, including Caregiving in the context of HIV/AIDS (http://www.un.org/womenwatch/daw/csw/53sesspriorityhtm.htm).

There is less activity around what Sylvia Chant calls "defeminization of gender planning," or efforts to pull gender out of ghettoized departments and really transform institutional culture to bring gender into the mainstream (Chant 2000: 12). We would add that in addition to pulling more men (and male perspectives) into GAD work, gender specialists should also specialize in and be incorporated into other areas of development policy and planning, serving for instance as economists, bankers, public health administrators and agricultural extension agents. As long as gender is a sort of add-on or reaction to economic development theory, planning, or practice, it will never be treated as the structural foundation of economic development that it really is.

CHAPTER 3 **STATISTICAL OVERVIEW**

In this section we provide a statistical description of the world's women and men in the context of economic development, presented primarily by population-weighted regional averages. Our coverage is not exhaustive in the sense of including every available measure of gender and economic development, but rather representative, intended to give readers a sense of the statistics available and what these indicate about the state of gender equality and the well-being of women and men.

When dealing with gender-aware statistics, one must choose what we variously term perspective, dimension and methodology. Perspective refers to whether one is measuring absolute achievements or gender equality. Statistics on absolute achievements involve looking at how economic development has affected women's and men's absolute levels of well-being. Some further qualify achievements by differentiating between capabilities, a state of well-being, and opportunities, which constitute chances to enhance one's own or others' well-being. Conversely, equality measures capture women's versus men's relative achievements, regardless of absolute well-being or level of development (e.g. a country could have complete gender equality in literacy but literacy levels could be low).[2] Some gender statistics mix absolute with equality measurements, such as the UN's Gender and Development Index, discussed more fully below.

Dimension refers to the topical content of the statistic, such as the human capability of life expectancy versus the economic opportunity of paid labor force participation. The most challenging dimension issue is limited data coverage. While scholars and practitioners may conclude that using measures of the gender-based wage gap, time use or physical security are essential to portraying gender dynamics, there just is not the country or time series coverage to include these components in most developing country-level studies, much less studies that are global in scope.

The last issue is methodology, and while the list of statistical challenges and choices is long and somewhat esoteric for the non-statistician, we differentiate here only between using indicators versus indices. Indicators measure only one dimension, such as percent of parliament seats or employment to population ratio. Indices combine a number of indicators to construct a composite measure. We cover both indicators and indices below.

The overview is subdivided into three sections. The first section on employment indicators covers work and the labor market, with some discussion of the economic explanations for these gender differences. The second section presents the data used to track Millennium Development Goal 3 (MDG3), "to promote gender equality and empower women," as the MDGs (and their associated targets and indicators) are such a central feature of contemporary development dialogues.

---

2 Note that we have not used the term "empowerment" in either the absolute or relative dynamic description, as the term is (sometimes confusingly) used to refer to both absolute and relative achievements.

The third section gives an overview of gendered indices, focusing primarily on the UN's Gender Development Index (GDI) and Gender Empowerment Measure (GEM), but including a number of others for comparison as well.

3.1 Employment Indicators

Figure 1 illustrates adult employment-to-population ratios by sex and region in 1998 and 2006 based on International Labour Organization (ILO) estimates. These ratios exclude youth (aged 15-24) to control for the effects of regional and longitudinal differences in youth education on labor force participation. These figures are also intended to capture informal workers and unpaid family workers, though these categories of workers are undoubtedly undercounted in labor force and census surveys, and because women constitute a higher proportion of these categories than men around the world, they are more likely to be undercounted than men. We present employment-to-population ratios rather than labor force participation rates to capture the proportion of the population that is actually employed. Figure 2 presents unemployment rates by sex and region for the same time period to give readers a sense of labor force participants that are actively looking for but cannot find work.

Looking at figure 1, we see that women's employment is lower than men's across all regions and levels of development, though there is a lot of variation in the gendered employment gap. The biggest gaps are in the Middle East and North Africa, followed by South Asia; the smallest in East Asia, followed by Central and South Eastern Europe, the Developed Economies and the European Union. At the macroeconomic level, economists explain gender differences in labor force participation primarily by controlling for income per capita, fertility, whether the economy is primarily agricultural, and region

(see Clark, York and Anker (2003) for an example). The conventional wisdom, borne out by a number of empirical studies, is that female labor force participation tends to follow a U-shaped pattern as development proceeds and incomes increase: high in the early stages of development and industrialization when women's roles in traditional modes of production are significant, declining in the middle stages of industrialization as household incomes rise and new industrial sectors displace women's roles in traditional production, and rising once again in the later stages of industrialization as service sectors expand along with the demand for women's market labor (and the rising opportunity cost of not working for pay). Independent of income, economies dominated by traditional agriculture also tend to have higher female labor force participation all else equal – hence the high female employment rates in Sub-Saharan Africa despite low income per capita. Fertility is used as a proxy for the extent to which the demands of family constrain female labor force participation, though the effect can also run the other way: better opportunities in the labor market draw women out of the home and lower fertility. Controlling for regional differences – independent of per capita income, size of the agricultural sector, and fertility – is variously used as a control for the gender culture, preferences, or any other factor common within a region that is not explicitly measured in the study. So, for instance, female labor force participation rates in the Middle East and North Africa are lower than predicted by their per capita income, fertility, and agricultural sectors, an outcome that many attribute to a gender culture that discourages market work for women. Conversely, East Asia has higher female labor force participation rates than the empirical model would predict, a result not attributed to the gender culture but rather the female labor-intensive export-oriented development model adopted by many East Asian countries (Standing 1989).

FIGURE 1: **Adult employment-to-population ratios, by sex and region, 1998 and 2008 (percent)**

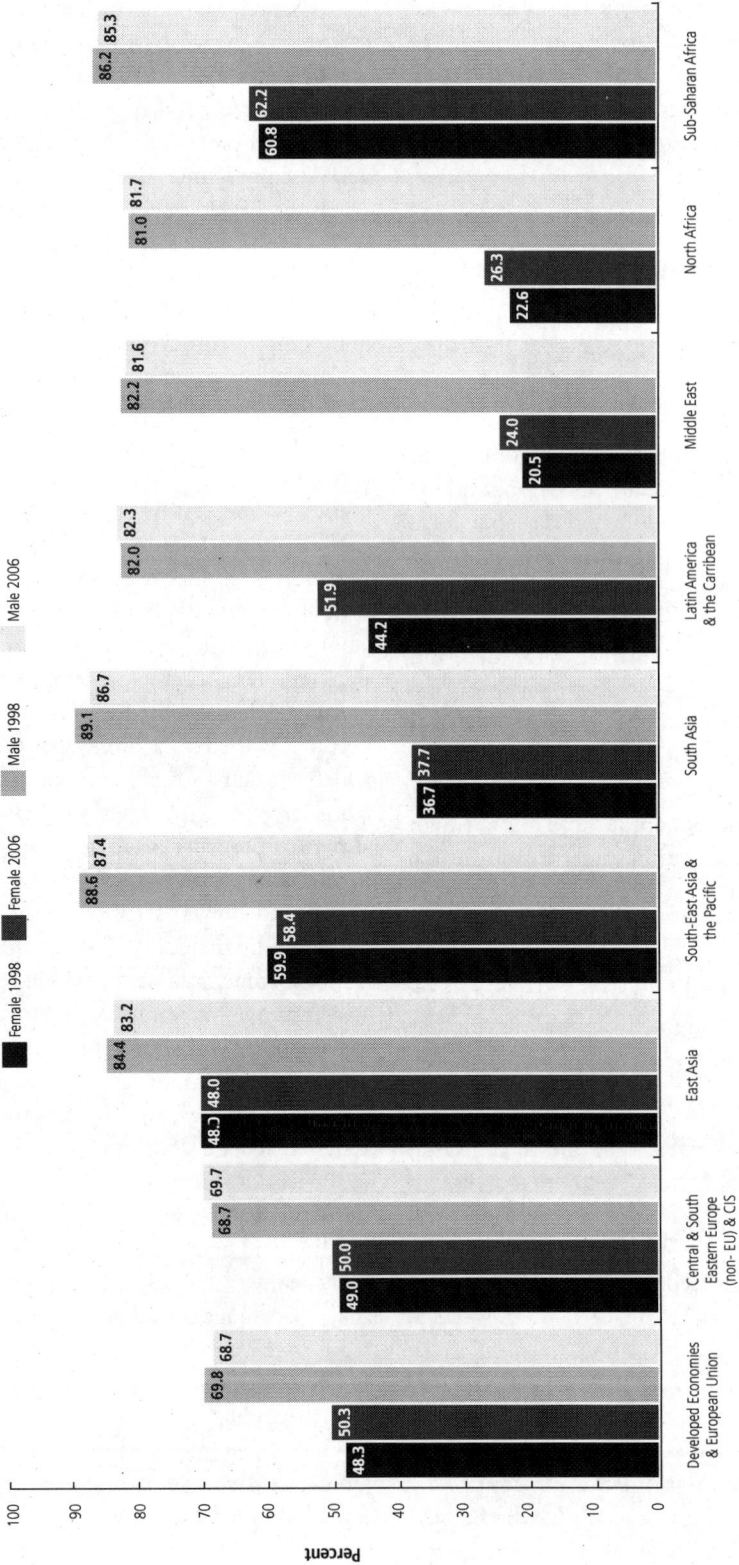

Legend: Female 1998 | Female 2006 | Male 1998 | Male 2006

Developed Economies & European Union: 69.8, 68.7, 50.3, 48.3

Central & South Eastern Europe (non- EU) & CIS: 69.7, 68.7, 50.0, 49.0

East Asia: 83.2, 84.4, 48.0, 48.3

South-East Asia & the Pacific: 87.4, 88.6, 58.4, 59.9

South Asia: 86.7, 89.1, 37.7, 36.7

Latin America & the Carribean: 82.3, 82.0, 51.9, 44.2

Middle East: 81.6, 82.2, 24.0, 20.5

North Africa: 81.7, 81.0, 26.3, 22.6

Sub-Saharan Africa: 85.3, 86.2, 62.2, 60.8

Percent

Source: ILO. 2009. Global Employment Trends for Women. Geneva: ILO, Table A5.
Notes: Figures exclude youths aged 15-24. Figures estimated by the ILO using its Global Employment Trends Model, which employs econometric methods to produce regional estimates of labor market indicators when country data is unavailable.

Still, there are some commonalities across regions. Turning back to figure 1, we see that women's and men's employment-to-population ratios are converging around the world, with the exception of South-East Asia and the Pacific (where employment rates have diverged a little over 0.3 percentage points between 1998 and 2006). The largest convergence by far is in Latin America and the Caribbean, where women's employment-to-population ratio increased by 7.7 percentage points, compared to a 0.3 percentage point increase in men's ratio. In most cases, except for Central and South Eastern Europe, Latin America and the Caribbean, and North Africa, convergence between women's and men's employment rates is both the result of increases in women's employment and declines in men's employment.[3]

Since these figures illustrate employment rather than labor force participation, it could be that men's employment is declining in most regions because of increased difficulty in finding work relative to women, or because of non-labor market factors, such as earlier retirement or higher rates of disability (recall that figure 1 illustrates adult employment, so spending more time in formal education will not affect the figures very much). We turn to figure 2 to indicate whether this is indeed the case. Women's unemployment rates are higher than men's in all regions in both 1998 and 2006, with the notable exception of East Asia in both 1998 and 2006, and Central and South Eastern Europe in 2006 only. The gender gap in unemployment (with women having higher unemployment rates than men), and absolute level of unemployment, is most pronounced in Latin America and the Caribbean and the Middle East and North Africa, while the gender gap is most narrow among developed economies.

For the most part, then, these figures do not suggest that women are making employment gains at the expense of men's employment, though a more disaggregated and country-specific analysis is necessary to assert this claim more strongly.[4]

What about the 2008 financial crisis and the consequent global recession in 2008/09? Advanced economies were hit harder than the developing world in terms of aggregate GDP growth. Advanced economy output grew by 0.5 percent in 2008 and declined by 3.2 percent in 2009; the figures for emerging and developing countries are increases of 6.1 and 2.1 percent in 2008 and 2009 respectively (IMF 2010). While we do not have regional unemployment estimates for this period, we can make some preliminary observations based on individual reporting from national labour force surveys. Some countries in the developed world have experienced much wider dispersion in sex-specific unemployment rates than prior to the recession, with men's unemployment increasing much faster than women's in the United Kingdom, Iceland, Ireland, and the United States and Canada.[5] This is a result of the fact that some of the hardest hit industries in these countries, such as banking, finance, and construction, are male-dominated industries.

Turning to the emerging and developing economies, based on the data available, there is no marked divergence from the gendered unemployment patterns in the developing world relative to before the recession, and indeed, there seems to be much less recession-induced unemployment relative to the advanced economies, as the figures on economic growth suggest.[6]

---

3 Of course, it could also be that the labor market surveys and census data used by the ILO to generate these estimates are getting better at recording women's market work, though the statistical techniques used by the ILO, which include time series information, should minimize this effect.

4 The latest year in figures 1 and 2 is 2006, although estimates are available from the ILO up through 2008. It is this author's opinion that the ILO model probably underestimates the impact of the global recession on employment, and so we do not report these later estimates.

5 This conclusion is based on unemployment rates reported to the ILO and published as part of their global statistics on the labour market series: http://www.ilo.org/pls/apex/f?p=109:1:0.

6 See footnote 4 for source.

FIGURE 2: **Unemployment Rate by Sex & Region, 1998 & 2006**

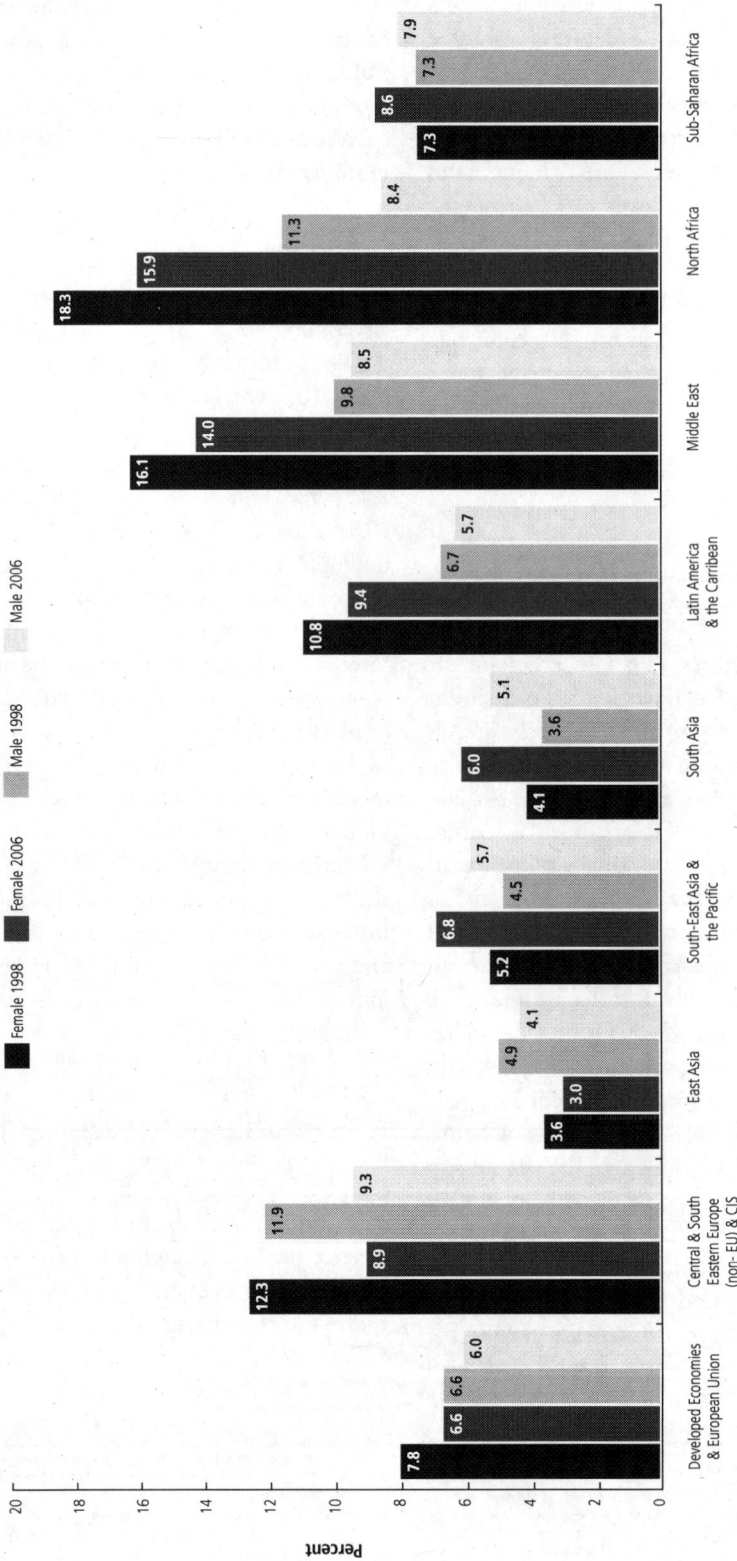

Legend: ■ Female 1998 ■ Female 2006 ▨ Male 1998 ▨ Male 2006

Region	Female 1998	Female 2006	Male 1998	Male 2006
Developed Economies & European Union	7.8	6.6	6.6	6.0
Central & South Eastern Europe (non-EU) & CIS	12.3	8.9	11.9	9.3
East Asia	3.6	3.0	4.9	4.1
South-East Asia & the Pacific	5.2	6.8	4.5	5.7
South Asia	4.1	6.0	3.6	5.1
Latin America & the Carribean	10.8	9.4	6.7	5.7
Middle East	16.1	14.0	9.8	8.5
North Africa	18.3	15.9	11.3	8.4
Sub-Saharan Africa	7.3	8.6	7.3	7.9

Source: ILO. 2009. Global Employment Trends for Women. Geneva: ILO, Table A2.
Notes: Figures estimated by the ILO using its Global Employment Trends Model,
which employs econometric methods to produce regiona. estimates of labor
market indicators when country data is unavailable.

But capturing the impact of the global recession using standard macroeconomic indicators like GDP growth and unemployment rates in developing economies is potentially misleading on a couple of counts. First, owing to the greater likelihood of informal and insecure work in developing countries relative to advanced economies, it is more likely that unemployed developing economy workers will move out of standard labor categories and not be counted as officially unemployed during periods of economic upheaval. Second, social safety nets that provide benefits like unemployment insurance and food for the poor are weak to non-existent in the developing world, so even seemingly small increases in unemployment can have extremely deleterious impacts on human development relative to the social dislocation experienced in advanced economies as a result of unemployment.

One way to get at this issue is to consider the ILO's figures on the share of what it terms "vulnerable employment", which refers to the sum of own-account workers and contributing family workers as a share of total employment. Workers in vulnerable employment face greater economic risk; they are less likely to have formal work arrangements and access to social insurance, while earning less income and facing more income volatility overall (ILO 2009). Looking at figure 3, we see that the majority of workers are engaged in vulnerable employment in most developing regions, with the exception of Latin America and the Caribbean, the Middle East and North Africa. In addition, women are more likely to experience this vulnerability in every region except for Latin America and the Caribbean, where men's and women's shares are very close. Clearly, to the extent that these shares represent the distribution of economic insecurity between women and men, women's employment is on the whole certainly more unstable and hence more vulnerable to the vagaries of the economic boom-and-bust cycle.

It is not just whether one has a job that contributes to economic well-being, but also the income earned from that work. Figure 4 illustrates the percentage gender gap in median earnings of full-time employees for OECD countries. It is good to consider median, as opposed to average, earnings because the median is not influenced by extremely high (pulling the average up) or low earners (pulling the average down). One is essentially considering what the middle person in the spectrum of earners is earning. The average median gap among OECD countries is 17.6 percent. That is, among full-time workers, men earn 17.6 percent more than women on average when considering median earnings. This average masks some large differences between countries, however, with Korea and Japan showing a 38.0 percent and 33.0 percent gap respectively, followed by Germany at 23.0 percent.

Gender-specific wage data is notoriously spotty and at times misleading when it does exist for developing economies. For example, wage gaps tend to be lower in regions that are associated with the greatest gender inequalities in other measures such as education or labor force participation (e.g. countries in the Middle East and North Africa, Sub-Saharan Africa, and low-income Asian countries) (Tzannatos 2009). This is because women in the labor market in these countries are those with more education and thus relatively high labor market returns; women in these regions are also more likely than men to be working for the higher-paying public sector (Ibid.). That said, we can make some general statements about the gender pay gap and women's income in the context of economic development. Women typically earn about two-thirds of what similar men earn, with only around 20 percent of the world's wages accruing to women – both because women are less likely to work for pay than men, and because when they do work for pay, they tend to work in low-paying sectors (Ibid: 154).

FIGURE 3: **Vulnerable Employment Share by Sex and Region, 2007 (percent)**

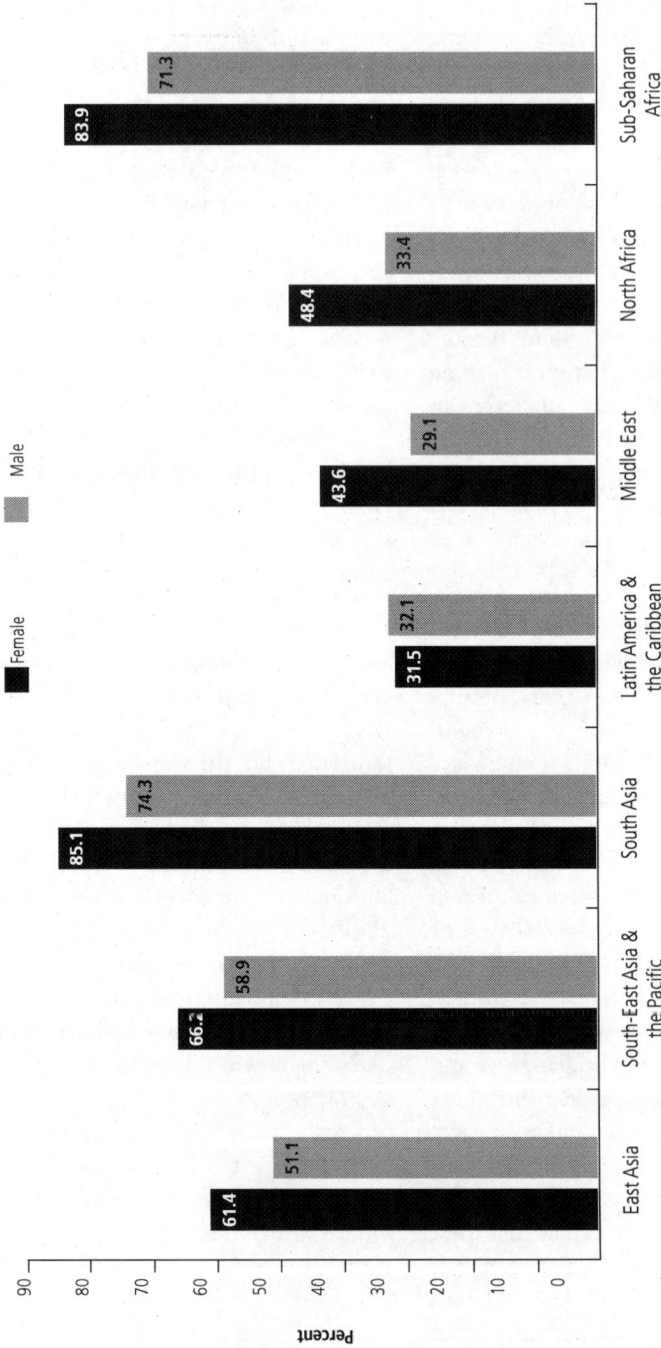

	Female	Male
East Asia	61.4	51.1
South-East Asia & the Pacific	66.2	58.9
South Asia	85.1	74.3
Latin America & the Caribbean	31.5	32.1
Middle East	43.6	29.1
North Africa	48.4	33.4
Sub-Saharan Africa	83.9	71.3

Source: ILO. 2009. Global Employment Trends for Women. Geneva: ILO, Table A7.
Note: Vulnerable employment refers to the sum of own account workers and contributing family workers as a share of total employment.

This suggests that the sorting of women and men into different occupations and industries – referred to as sex segregation – contributes to the gender wage gap. Even in the aggregate, segregation by sex is apparent. Figure 5 illustrates the sectoral distribution of employment by sex and region for 1998 and 2008, and a couple of patterns appear. The service sector is by far the largest source of both women's and men's employment for the Developed Economies, Central and South Eastern Europe, and Latin America and the Caribbean, though women have a larger and increasing share of employment in the service sector relative to men for all three regions. A similar point can be made about the agricultural sector in South Asia and Sub-Saharan Africa: it is the largest (but declining) source of employment for both women and men, though its share of employment declined faster between 1998 and 2008 for men than for women. Industry is a more significant source of employment for men than women throughout the world, though the industrial share is similar for women and men in East and South East Asia.

The less aggregated the industry or occupation, the more sex segregation there is, a phenomenon that does not seem to change much with economic development (Clark, York and Anker 2003). In export-oriented industrial production, for instance, it is well-documented that women are concentrated in the most labor-intensive sectors, garments and electronics, while men are more likely to work in more capital intensive, higher value-added (and paying) industrial sectors (Braunstein and Brenner 2007; Çagatay 2001; Elson 1996; Fontana 2009). Female-dominated industries and occupations have different career ladders and structures of pay even when productivity characteristics like education and skill are the same (Tzannatos 2009: 147-48). As documented by the statistics on vulnerable employment in figure 3, women are also more likely to work in the informal sector,

or to be a temporary, part-time or casual worker in the home or subcontracting (Ibid.). Women also tend to be concentrated in fewer professions than men. In a cross-country study of gender and the labor market, Clark, York and Anker (2003) found seven times as many male-dominated occupations as female-dominated occupations. So men face little competition from women in most sectors of the labor market, and women's crowding into fewer occupations depresses wages in female-dominated occupations while raising them in male-dominated occupations.

3.2 Millennium Development Goals Indicators

Dissatisfaction with the economic performance of the 1980s and the 1990s led world leaders from 189 countries to adopt the MDGs in 2000, a set of eight goals to address poverty by 2015 (Grown 2008a). The target for MDG Goal 3, to "promote gender equality and empower women," is to "eliminate gender disparity in primary and secondary education, preferably by 2005, and in all levels of education no later than 2015" (UN 2009: 18). Eighty-two out of 122 countries (with data available) achieved the mid-term target of parity in primary and secondary schooling by 2005. Only one additional country is on track to achieve it by 2015. Around 19 countries seem unlikely to achieve this target by 2015; of these, 13 are in Sub-Saharan Africa (Buvinic and Morrison 2008: 9).

Many have critiqued this target as too narrow a definition of gender equality and empowerment, and have advocated a sort of "MDG-plus" approach that supplements the education target with a number of other strategic priorities dealing with issues like sexual and reproductive health and rights, property rights, violence and social infrastructure (Buvinic and Morrison 2008; Grown, Gupta, and Aslihan 2005).

FIGURE 4: **Percentage Gender Gap in Median Earnings of Full-Time Employees in OECD Countries, 2006 or latest year available**

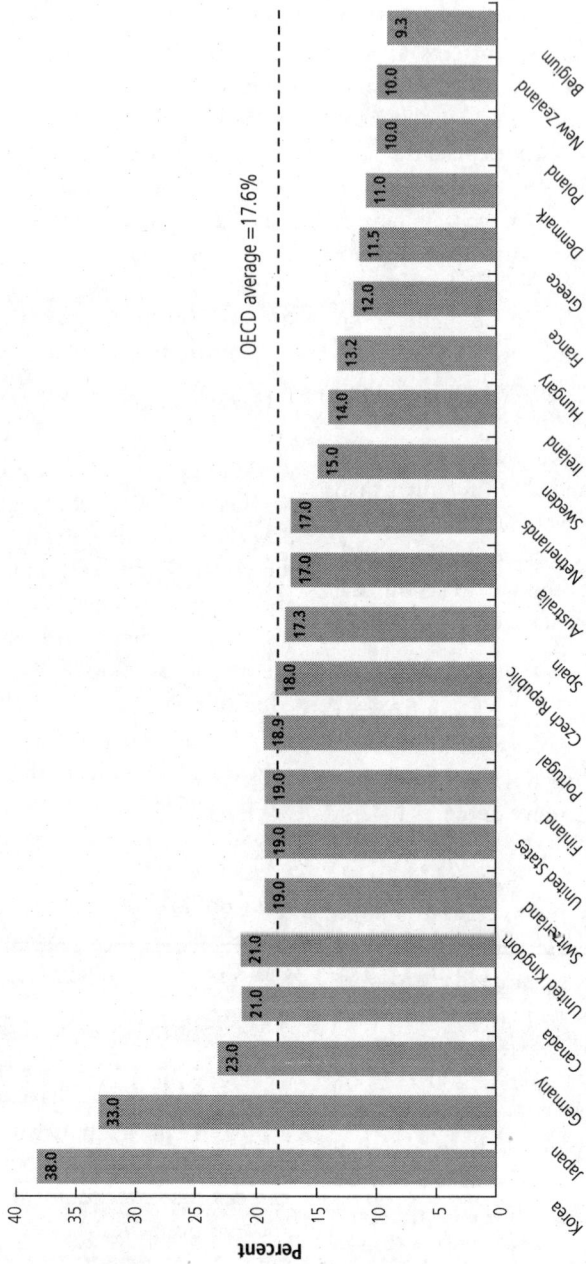

Country	Percent
Korea	38.0
Japan	33.0
Germany	23.0
Canada	21.0
United Kingdom	21.0
Switzerland	19.0
United States	19.0
Finland	19.0
Portugal	18.9
Czech Republic	18.0
Spain	17.3
Australia	17.0
Netherlands	17.0
Sweden	15.0
Ireland	14.0
Hungary	13.2
France	12.0
Greece	11.5
Denmark	11.0
Poland	10.0
New Zealand	10.0
Belgium	9.3

OECD average =17.6%

Source: Organisation for Economic Cooperation and Development.

But in light of the dominance of the MDGs in the development discourse, it is important to have a sense of the statistics used to evaluate MDG3 progress.

Three indicators are used to track MDG3: the ratio of girls to boys in primary, secondary and tertiary education; the share of women in wage employment in the nonagricultural sector, and the proportion of seats held by women in national parliament illustrates the education data by region for 2000 and 2007, and indicates that progress towards gender parity in all levels of education has been made over the period. For developing regions as a whole, in 2007 there were 95 girls per 100 boys enrolled in primary education, 94 in secondary education, and 96 in tertiary education. Though this progress is important, these ratios do not capture absolute enrollment rates (so increases could reflect lower enrollment for boys), nor do they indicate anything about completion rates, a perhaps more important indicator of the development of human capabilities (Buvinic and Morrison 2008.)

If we think of enrollment in school as an indicator of capabilities, and the share of women in non-agricultural wage employment and the proportion of seats held by women in parliaments as indicators of opportunities, there remains a lot more ground to be covered to reach gender parity in opportunities than capabilities, as illustrated by figures 6 and 7. The share of women in non-agricultural wage employment is a sort of reverse image of the vulnerable employment portrait in figure 3, as working for a wage outside of the agricultural sector indicates more stable, modern and higher-paid employment than other alternatives. With the exception of the Commonwealth of Independent States region, men constitute the majority of these workers in all regions, though the ratio is near 50 percent in developed regions (and the circumstances of other types of employment are not necessarily indicative of fewer opportunities for women in the same way as in developing regions).

For most regions, the share of women in non-agricultural wage employment roughly parallels women's employment-to-population ratios overall (see figure 1), with two exceptions: Sub-Saharan Africa and Southern Asia. In both of these regions, women are much more underrepresented in the modern wage sector – relative to their overall employment levels – than in other regions, as also suggested by their high shares of vulnerable employment in figure 3.

Turning to figure 8, for developing regions as a whole, women held 17.2 percent of national parliament seats as of January of 2009, compared with 10.8 percent in 2000. Women hold 30 percent or more of upper or lower national parliament chamber seats in 24 countries, and 30 percent or more of upper chamber seats in 15 countries (UN 2009: 23). These "frontrunners" are a diverse set of countries, and include developed countries as well as post-conflict and developing countries in Africa, Asia and Latin America and the Caribbean; nine chambers, mostly in the Pacific Islands and the Arab Gulf States, have no women members of parliament (Ibid.).

3.3 Composite Indices

Uni-dimensional indicators of gender differences, such as the ones reviewed above, are preferable when trying to understand a particular aspect of economic development. But the persistent use of, and dissatisfaction with, per capita GDP as a proxy for development has spurred the creation of composite indices to serve as an alternative. The earliest and most well-known is the UNDP's Human Development Index (HDI), which combines measures of health (life expectancy at birth), education (adult literacy and gross primary, secondary, and tertiary enrollment ratios), and standard of living (the natural log of per capita GDP at purchasing power parity). Regularly published with the UNDP's annual *Human Development Report*

FIGURE 5: **Sectoral Distribution of Employment by Sex and Region, 1998 & 2008**

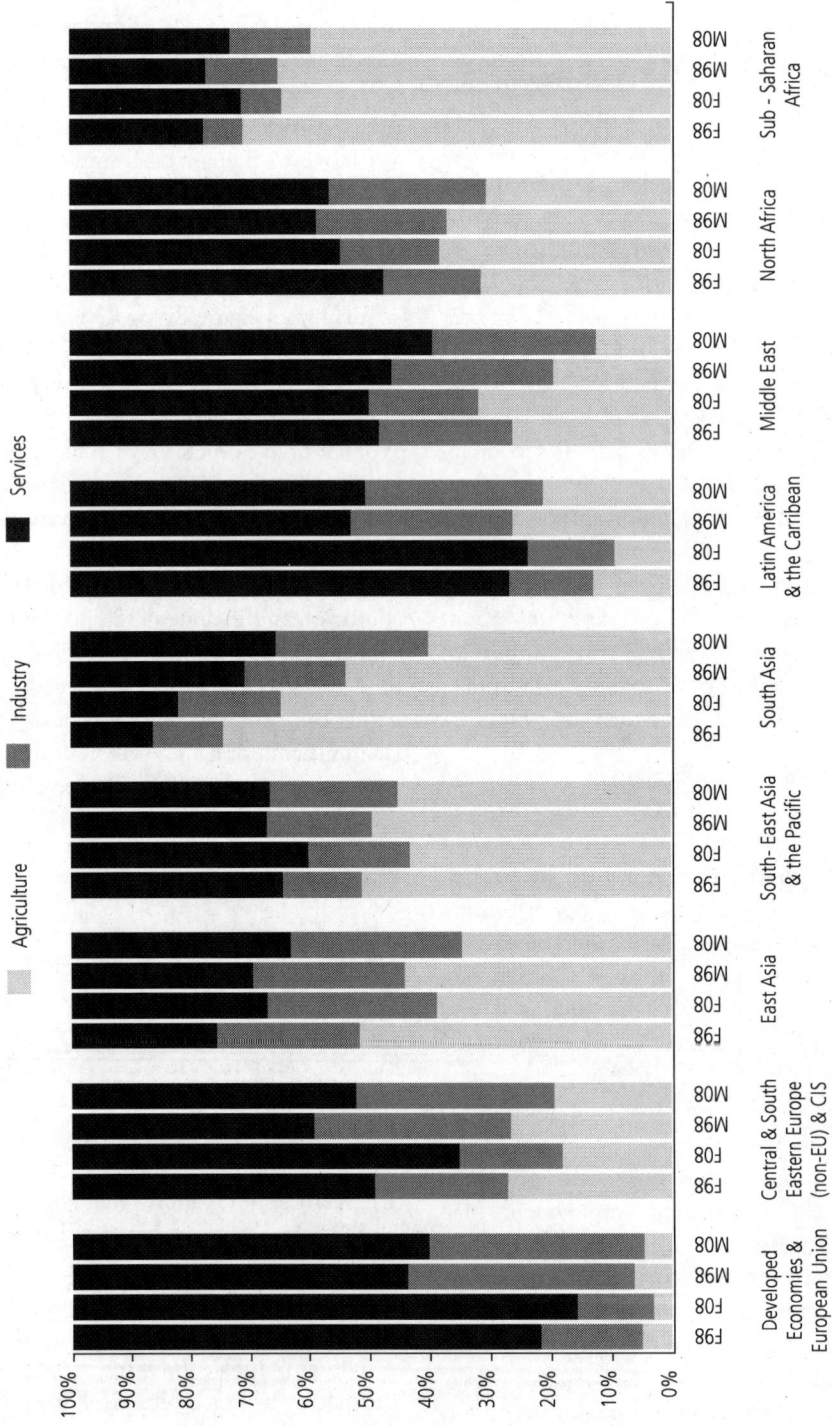

Source: ILO. 2009. Global Employment Trends for Women. Geneva: ILO, Tables A6b and A6c.
Note: F98 refers to females in 1998, F08 to females in 2008, and M98 and M08 to male shares in 1998 and 2008 respectively.

FIGURE 6: **Ratios of girls to boys in primary, secondary and tertiary education (girls per 100 boys)**

(a) Primary education

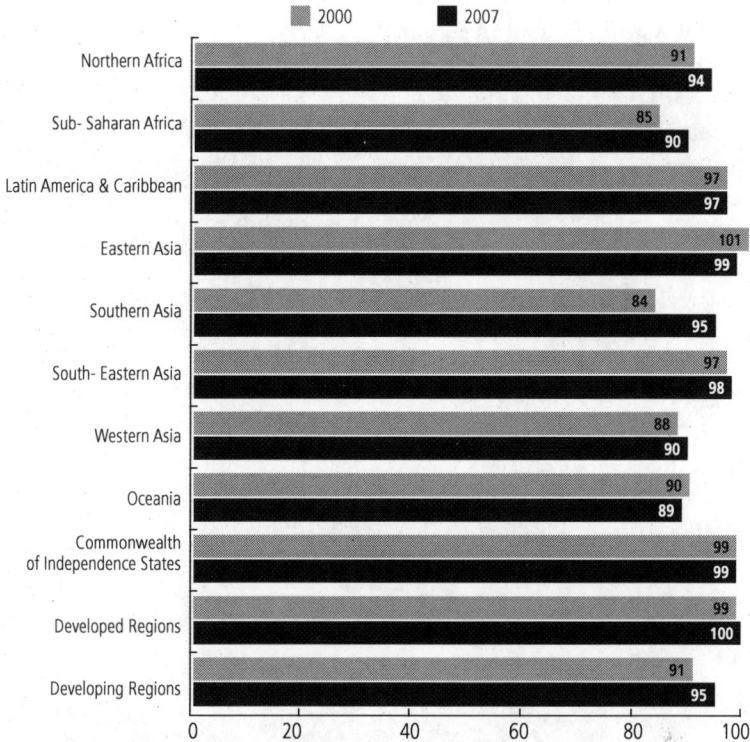

since 1990, the HDI reflects Amartya Sen's work on the centrality of functionings and capabilities as the appropriate target and barometer of development efforts.

The 1995 *Human Development Report* introduced two new human development indicators: the gender development indicator (GDI) and the gender empowerment measure (GEM). The GDI imposes a welfare penalty on the HDI for differences between men and women in life expectancy, adult illiteracy and gross enrollment ratios (what proportion of the age-appropriate population is enrolled in primary, secondary, and tertiary education), and earned income. The GEM combines measures of women's relative empowerment in

the following three areas: political participation and decision-making, as reflected in women's and men's percentage shares of parliamentary seats; economic participation and decision-making, as measured by women's relative share of positions as legislators, senior officials, managers, and professional and technical workers; and power over economic resources, as measured by their share of earned income (UN 2007: 360).

Both the GDI and the GEM have spawned a number of comparative studies, debate, and the creation of new, alternative aggregate measures of gender inequality and absolute achievements (see the *Journal of Human Development's* 2006 special issue for an overview of this work). One of the more common criticisms is that the GDI is sometimes used incorrectly as a stand-alone measure of gender inequality, when it was designed to be used in direct comparison to the HDI to underscore the GDI's role as a welfare penalty to the HDI (Grown 2008b). A second critique applies to the statistical methodology used to compute both the GDI and the GEM. For both indices, the component with the most variation (income) ends up having the most influence, so the indices mix measures of gender equality with measures of absolute well-being, and women in wealthier countries appear to have greater gender equality when they actually have similar shares of economic or political power as women in lower income countries (Dijkstra 2006; Grown 2008b). This is sometimes referred to as a "weighting problem," because high variance components of the index end up with greater weights than low variance components. A third issue is that

most indices are based on some average of their components, so high gender equality in one area can mute extreme gender inequality in another. The ultimate question is how to interpret the final index.

With these caveats in mind, we illustrate the latest figures for the HDI, GDI and GEM by region in figure 9. Note that none of the regions incur a very high human development welfare penalty when comparing the HDI and the GDI. One way to capture this relationship is by using the ratio of the GDI to the HDI; a ratio of one means that there is no welfare penalty for gender inequality in human development. Table 2 gives these ratios by region, with the lowest ratio in the Arab States being 0.967, and the highest in the Central and Eastern European region at 0.998. Similar to the conditions suggested by the MDG3 education indicators, there is very limited gender inequality in capabilities

(b) Secondary education

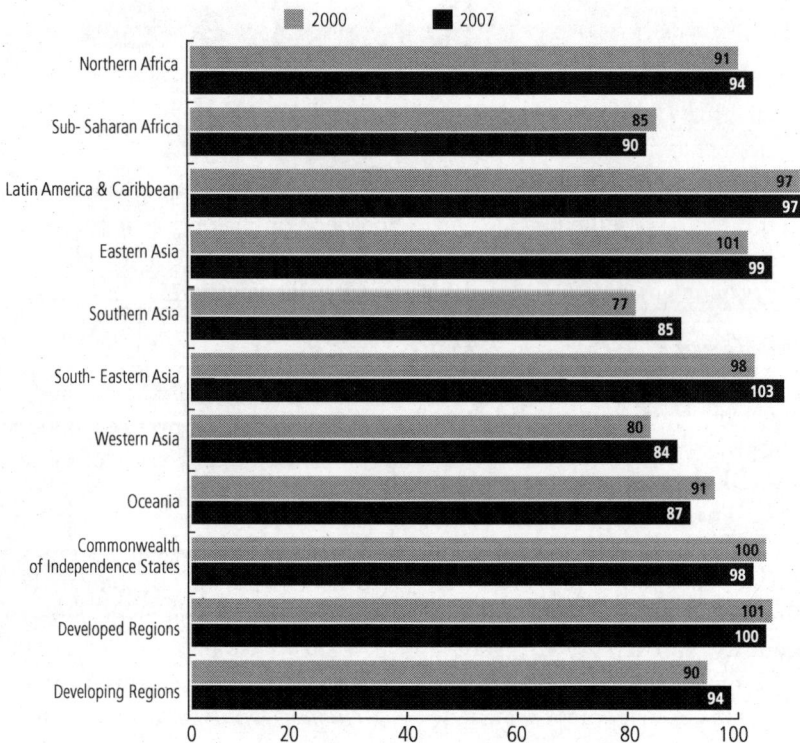

(c) Tertiary education

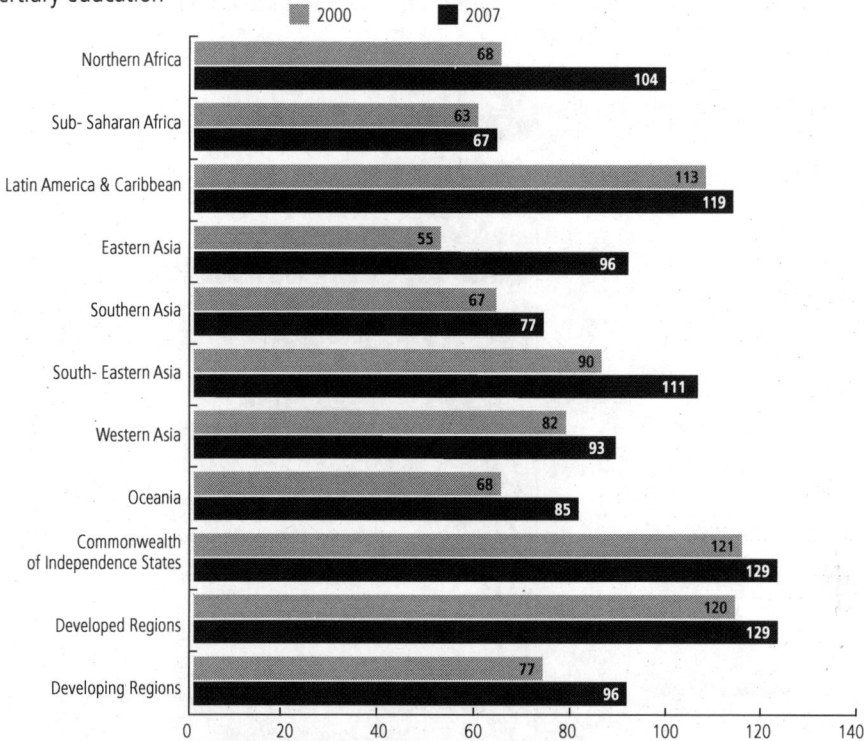

Legend: ▥ 2000   ■ 2007

Region	2000	2007
Northern Africa	68	104
Sub-Saharan Africa	63	67
Latin America & Caribbean	113	119
Eastern Asia	55	96
Southern Asia	67	77
South-Eastern Asia	90	111
Western Asia	82	93
Oceania	68	85
Commonwealth of Independence States	121	129
Developed Regions	120	129
Developing Regions	77	96

*Source: UN (2009), Statistical Annex. For a list of countries in each region, seehttp://mdgs.un.org/unsd/mdg/Host.
aspx?Content=Data/RegionalGroupings.htm.
Note: These ratios are based on gross enrollment: the number of girls and boys enrolled in a particular school level regardless of
age.*

as measured by comparing the HDI to the GDI (though there is a lot of variation in human development, as illustrated by the vertical differences in figure 9). The GEM, however, tells a slightly different story, with all regions scoring much lower on gendered empowerment than (gender inequality-adjusted) human development.

A number of scholars, practitioners and development organizations have come up with alternative composite measures that address the critiques of the GDI and the GEM. The following is a representative list.

- *The Standardized Index of Gender Equality* (SIGE) combines indicators that capture female versus male achievements in the following areas: education, life expectancy, economic activity rates, the female share of higher

labor market positions, and the female share of parliament (Dijkstra 2002). While all of these factors are reflected in the GDI and the GEM, the SIGE only captures the extent of gender equality (and not absolute achievements). It counters the weighting problem by standardizing the components of the index, so cross-country comparisons are more straightforward. But the standardization process means that gender inequality in any one country is measured relative to the average position of gender inequality in other countries, and does not indicate whether women's positions are better or worse than men's (Permanyer 2010). Another problem with this approach is that component weights are different every year, thus making comparisons over time somewhat problematic (Klasen 2006).

FIGURE 7: **Share of women in wage employment in the non-agricultural sector (percent)**

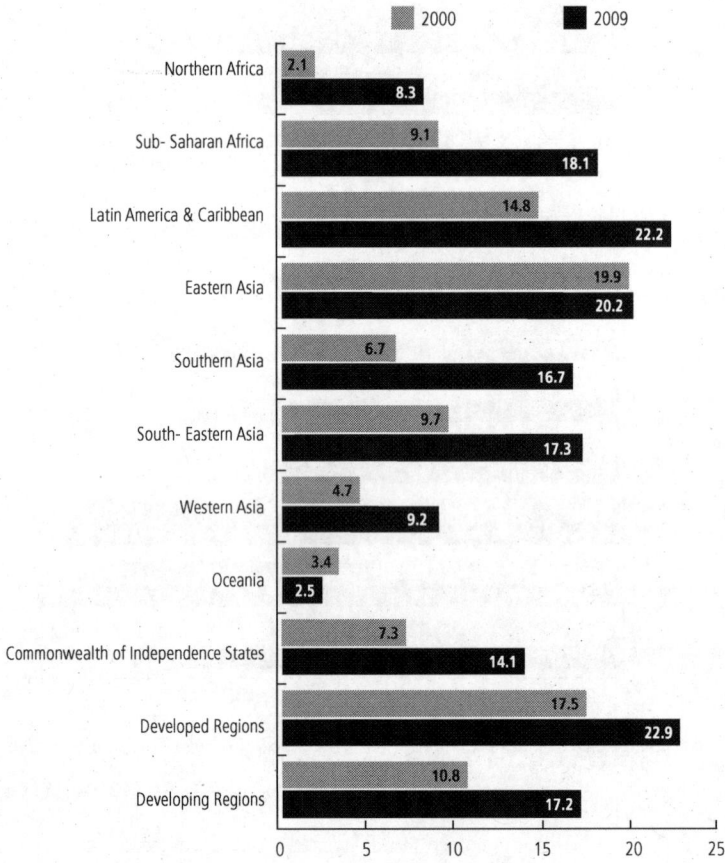

| | 2000 | 2009 |

Region	2000	2009
Northern Africa	2.1	8.3
Sub- Saharan Africa	9.1	18.1
Latin America & Caribbean	14.8	22.2
Eastern Asia	19.9	20.2
Southern Asia	6.7	16.7
South- Eastern Asia	9.7	17.3
Western Asia	4.7	9.2
Oceania	3.4	2.5
Commonwealth of Independence States	7.3	14.1
Developed Regions	17.5	22.9
Developing Regions	10.8	17.2

Source: Statistical Annex, U.N. (2009). For a list of countries in each region, see http://mdgs.un.org/unsd/mdg/Host. aspx?Content=Data/RegionalGroupings.htm.

TABLE 2: **Regional GDI as a proportion of HDI, 2007**

Developed & EU (non-CIS)	0.988
Central & Eastern Europe & CIS	0.998
East Asia & Pacific	0.996
South Asia	0.969
Arab States	0.967
Latin America & the Caribbean	0.994
Sub-Saharan Africa	0.980

Source: Author's calculations based on 2009 Human Development Report.

FIGURE 8: **Proportion of seats held by women in national parliament**

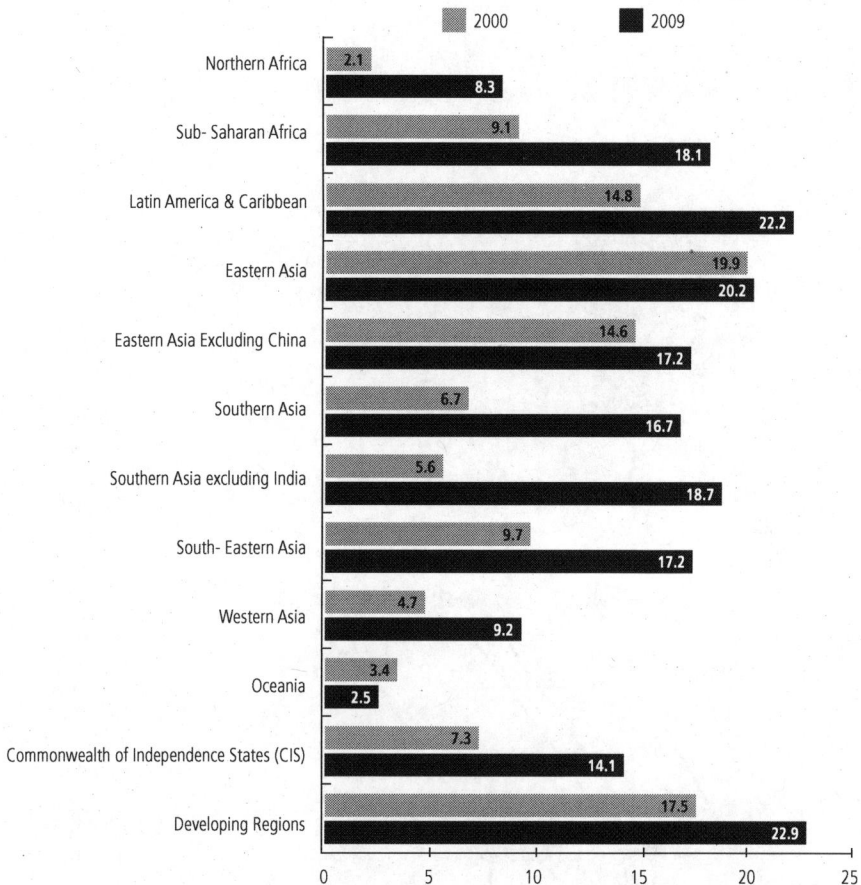

Source: Statistical Annex, U.N. (2009). For a list of countries in each region, see http://mdgs.un.org/unsd/mdg/Host.
aspx?Content=Data/RegionalGroupings.htm.

- *African Gender and Development Index.* Launched by the UN Economic Commission for Africa, the African GDI is an effort to broaden the scope of standard indices. It combines a Gender Status Index, which is a weighted average of the female-to-male ratio of 41 diverse indicators of basic capabilities, economic opportunities and political power, with the African Women's Progress Scoreboard, which uses 28 indicators to measure government policy performance in four areas: women's rights, capabilities, economic opportunities and political power (Grown 2008b; UNECA 2009).

The African GDI's strength – its broad coverage – is also its major weakness, as the data requirements mean it can be figured for only a limited number of countries (Permanyer 2010). A 2009 pilot study covered only 12 countries (UNECA 2009).

- *Social Watch Gender Equity Index (GEI).* Social Watch's GEI combines three composite measures of gender inequality, the components of which are measured as female-to-male ratios. Thus, it too measures female-to-male relative performance, not women's

FIGURE 9: **HDI, GDI and GEM by region, 2007**

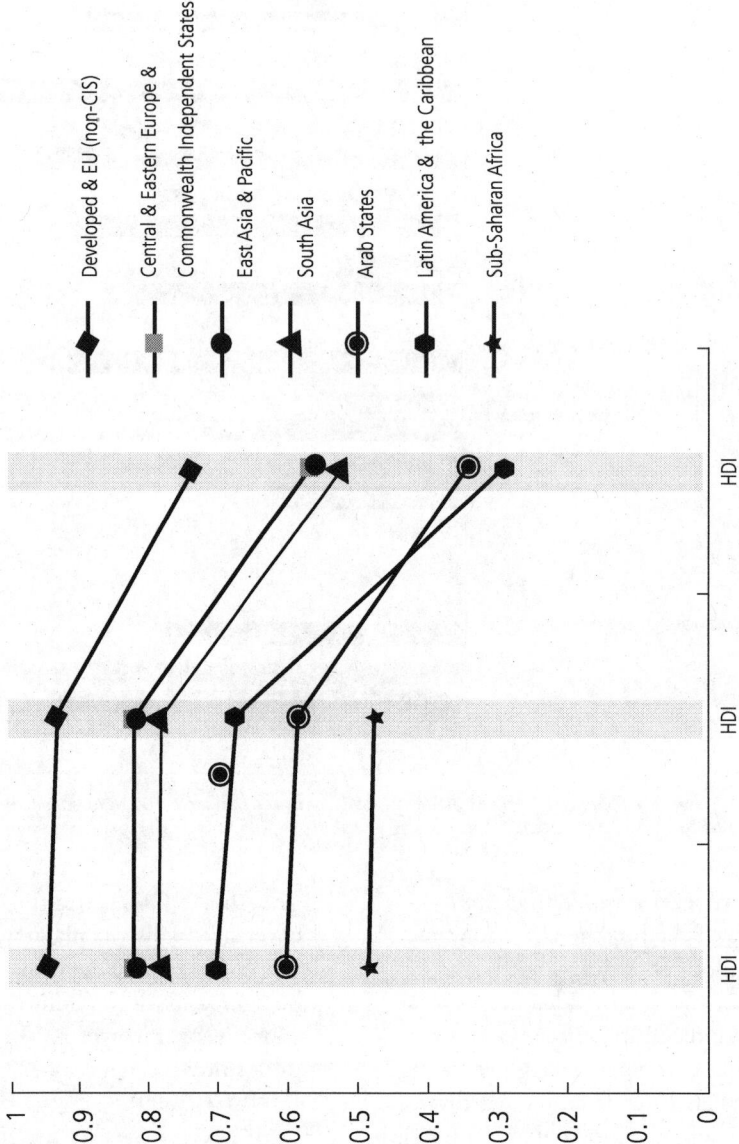

Source: Author's calculations based on data in the 2009 Human Development Report.
Notes: Indices are weighted by population. See Appendix A for a list of countries in each region, and how missing data were managed. There is no GEM observation for Sub-Saharan Africa due to lack of regional coverage.

or men's absolute achievements. The three areas include education, which is measured the same way as the GDI, economy, measured by the relative shares of income and total paid jobs, and empowerment, measured by relative shares in parliament, ministries, and higher labor market positions (Grown 2008b; Social Watch 2010). The result is a simple arithmetic average of the three dimensions, so high equality in one area compensates for low equality in another. And there is no standardization of the index components, so the indicator with the biggest variation will dominate the index (Grown 2008b).

- *Global Gender Gap Index.* The World Economic Forum's (WEF) Global Gender Gap Index (GGG) has been published annually since 2006, and it too captures relative achievements rather than women's absolute levels of empowerment. Its four components include: (1) economic participation and opportunity, which in addition to labor force participation, estimated income, and the proportion of women in higher end jobs, also includes an estimate of wage equality for similar work taken from the WEF's executive opinion survey; (2) educational attainment, which is the same as the GDI; (3) health and survival, which includes both life expectancy and sex ratios at birth, both adjusted for biological differences between women and men; and (4) political empowerment, which includes both the proportion of seats in higher levels of government and number of years with a female head of state. (Hausmann, Tyson and Zaahidi 2009). Sub-component values are weighted to correct for the problem of variables with highest variability having undue influence on the average, and then the four components are averaged together to get the GGG, with the maximum

score equal to one. As with the SIGE, weighting takes care of one problem and introduces another – that comparisons over time are problematic as the weights change each year.

To give readers an idea of what one of these alternative indices look like, figure 10 presents 2009 data on the WEF's GGG by region. While not directly comparable to the GDI or the GEM, it is still instructive to see an example of the different sorts of information portrayed by one of the alternative indicators. The GGG can be considered a sort of combination of the information represented by the GDI and the GEM, though the GGG focuses exclusively on female relative to male achievements, so it is more strictly comparable to the GEM. In terms of ordinal ranking, the GGG ordering roughly corresponds to the GEM ordering in figure 9, with the developed region at the top of the ranking, followed by Central and Eastern Europe and the Commonwealth Independent States, then East Asia and the Pacific and Latin America and the Caribbean (though Latin America ranks slightly above East Asia in the GEM ordering and slightly below in the GGG ordering), and finally by South Asia and the Arab States at the bottom (note there is no GEM observation for Sub-Saharan Africa due to limited data). The variance of the GEM is also higher, with a standard deviation (the standard difference between an observation and the entire group's average) of 0.16 compared to 0.05 for the GGG, perhaps because of the standardization process applied to the GGG computations.

Figure 11 illustrates the components of GGG by region in 2009 to give readers a sense of the relative performance of the components, and how averaging for an index can obscure information. Consistent with the MDG3 findings discussed above, gender equality is greatest in the capabilities of education and health in all regions. The next highest category (though with far lower scores than education and health) is economic participation and

FIGURE 10: **The Global Gender Gap Index by region, 2009**

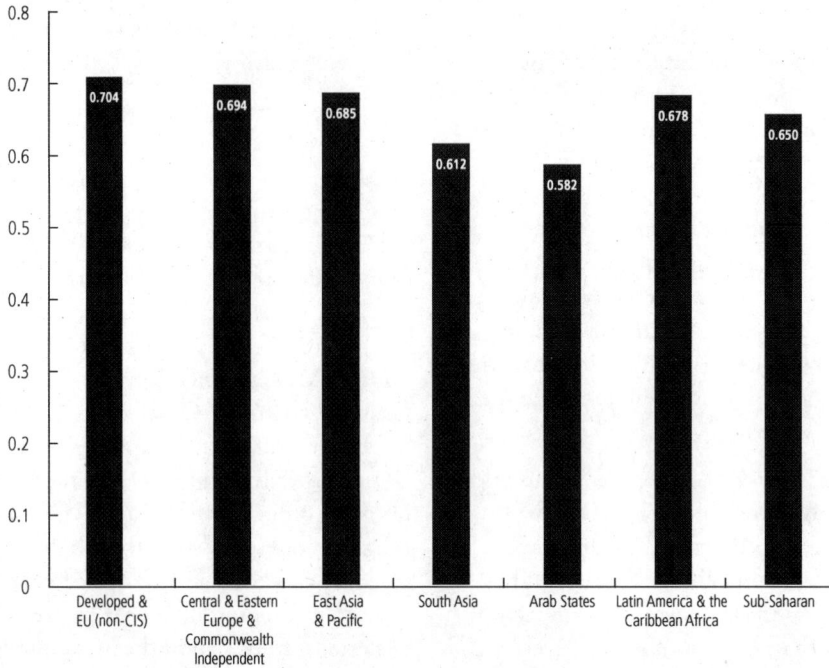

Source: Author's calculations based on data from Haussman, Tyson and Zahidi (2009).
Note: Regional grouping scores weighted by population. See Appendix A for a list of countries of in regional groupings, and further notes on the weighting scheme.

opportunity, with South Asia and the Arab States ranking lowest with scores of 0.41 and 0.42 respectively. As with the GEM, all regions lag farthest behind in terms of political empowerment, with South Asia ranking highest with a score of 0.25 (largely because of its tradition of female heads of state), followed by the developed region with a score of 0.19.

3.4 Summary

3.4.1 By Indicator

Employment Indicators

- In terms of adult employment-to-population ratios in 2006, men across the developing world have similarly high employment rates (with an average of 0.85), with lower rates in the developed and Central and Southeastern European regions (with an average of 0.69). They are, however, everywhere much higher than female employment rates. There are three categories of female adult employment-to-population ratios: low, medium and high. The Middle East and North Africa have similarly low female employment rates, with an average of 0.25. Medium female employment rates prevail in the developed economies, Central and South Eastern Europe, and Latin America and the Caribbean, with an average of 0.51. The highest female employment rates are found in East and South East Asia and Sub-Saharan Africa, with an average of 0.64.

FIGURE 11: **Components of the Global Gender Gap Index by Region, 2009**

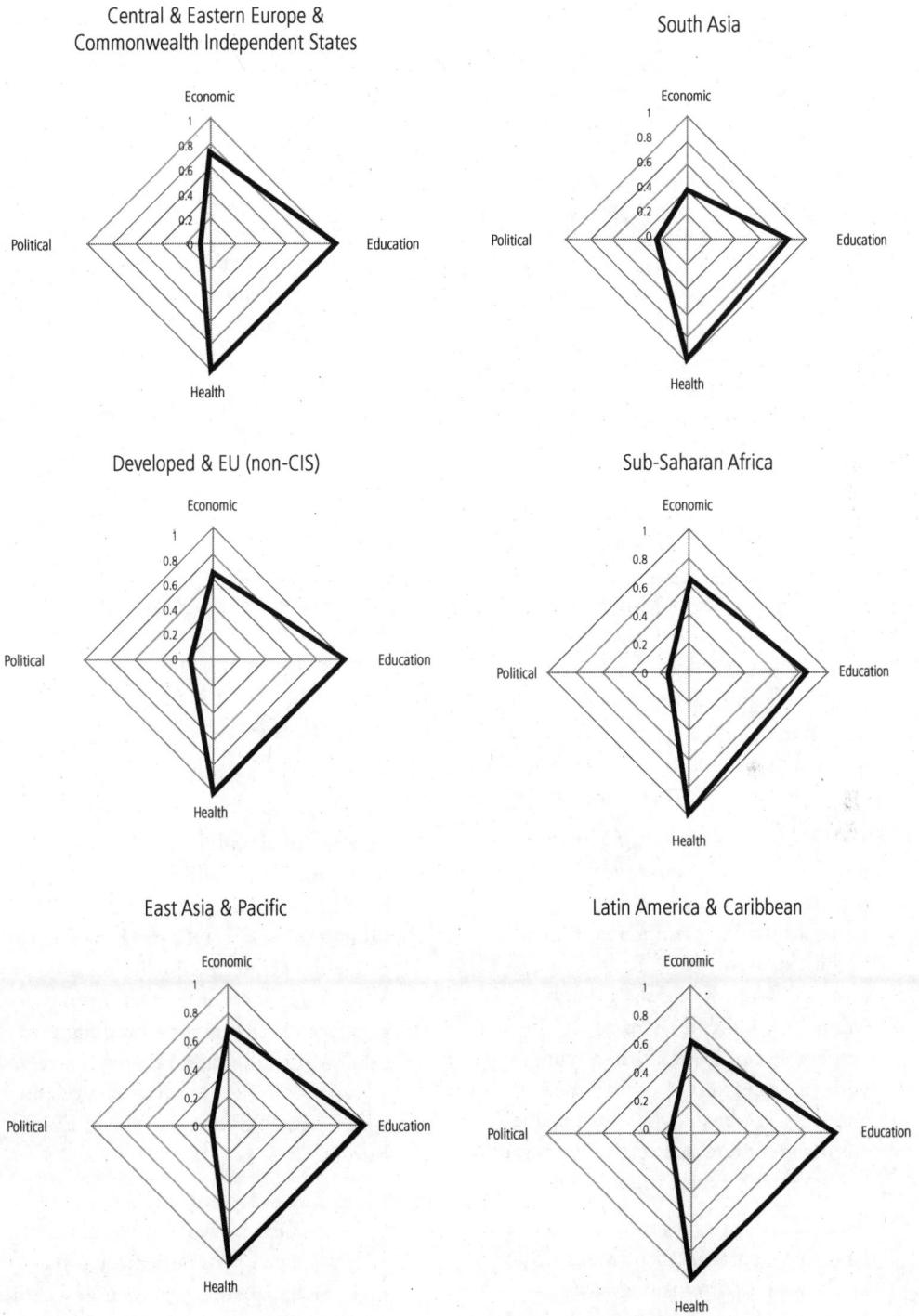

Central & Eastern Europe & Commonwealth Independent States

South Asia

Developed & EU (non-CIS)

Sub-Saharan Africa

East Asia & Pacific

Latin America & Caribbean

Arab States

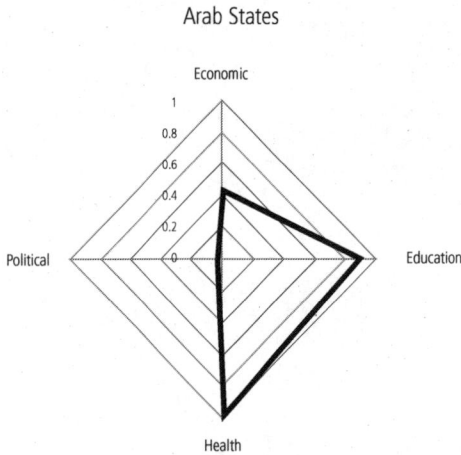

- Women face higher unemployment than men in all developing regions with the exception of East Asia, where women's unemployment rates are lower than men's (though unemployment rates are low for both groups overall). Women face particularly high unemployment rates in North Africa and the Middle East, where female unemployment was 18.3 percent and 16.1 percent respectively in 2006. Conversely, in developed regions men's unemployment has increased more than women's as a result of the 2008 financial crisis and consequent global recession.

- Vulnerable employment, defined as the sum of own account workers and contributing family workers, is the norm for working women and men in Sub-Saharan Africa, South Asia, East and South East Asia, though women are more likely to engage in vulnerable employment than men, with the exception of Latin America and the Caribbean, where vulnerable employment rates are relatively low and about equal for men and women.

- Available statistics reveal a lot more about labor force participation and aggregate employment patterns than gender-based wage gaps, sex segregation by industry or occupation, and the gender-

disaggregated impact of economic expansions and contractions. That said, available evidence indicates that jobs are extremely segregated by sex, and that women around the world earn less than men for similar work.

MDG3 Indicators

- MDG3 indicators portray the relative achievements of women and men in educational enrollments, wage employment, and parliamentary representation.

- At a regional level, women and men are near parity on capabilities as measured by gross enrollment in primary education; there is more inequality but significant convergence in secondary and tertiary education.

- A lot more ground remains to be covered in opportunities as measured by the female share of the wage labor force and seats in parliament.

Composite Indices

- The UNDP's GDI imposes a welfare penalty on the HDI for differences between men and women in life expectancy, adult illiteracy and gross enrollment ratios, and earned income. Using the GDI/HDI ratio is one way to gauge the gender inequality penalty on human development. Taken from that perspective, all regions scored high in 2007 – with the ratio ranging between a low of 0.967 for the Arab States and a high of 0.998 for Central and Eastern Europe.

- All regions score much lower on the UNDP's GEM – which reflects women's relative share of parliamentary seats, higher labor market positions and earned income –than on gender inequality-adjusted human development. The lowest ranking region is the Arab States with a score of 0.29 in 2007, followed closely by South Asia, with a score of 0.34. The highest score is for the developed economy region, at 0.73.

- Various scholars and development organizations have produced a number of alternatives to the GDI and the GEM in an attempt to address some of the methodological problems of and limited dimensions covered by the UNDP's indices.

- When disaggregating these indices, all regions score highest on the capability measures of education and health, followed by economic opportunity, with political participation consistently the most gender unequal component across all regions.

3.4.2 By Region

When development economists categorize the structures of developing economies, they generally refer to some or all of the following economic features: income level and size of the economy, physical and human resources, industrial structure, ethnic and religious composition, institutional and political structures, and historical background (Todaro and Smith 2006). Economies in the same region often share many of these traits, and so regional groupings are often used to present summary statistics and characterizations, as we have done in this statistical overview. In this sub-section, we discuss the statistical overview from a geographical perspective, characterizing how the various regions performed with regard to women and economic development and drawing out some themes that will be further addressed in the rest of the report.

East Asian countries have by far the highest female adult employment rates among all the regions, a result that is almost certainly determined largely by industrial structure and the emphasis on labor-intensive exports, which tends to raise demand for female labor. At the same time, this region also hosts some of the widest gender-based wage gaps in the world (as evidenced by figure 4), though China should be noted as an exception to this rule, a result of its historical commitment to gender wage parity (Braunstein and Brenner 2007). At the same time, there is gender parity in education and health measures, so a portrait of women being integrated in economic development, albeit on unequal terms, emerges. Indeed, a number of scholars have argued that women's high human capital, high labor force participation and low wages has been a key aspect of East Asia's development successes (Amsden 1989; Seguino 2000a).

South-East Asia and Sub-Saharan Africa are sometimes grouped together as regions that have historically high female labor force participation and large agricultural sectors, but the regions are really very different. South-East Asia's industrial structure has become much more service- and industry-intensive relative to Sub-Saharan Africa, though the vulnerable employment share is still extremely high by developing economy standards (66.2 percent for women and 58.9 percent for men), suggesting a significant informal sector despite a robust decade of real economic growth, which averaged 6.9 percent between 2000 and 2008.[7] Women's enrollment rates are higher than men's at all levels of education in South-East Asia (see figure 5), as well as being high in absolute terms.

---

7 *Average calculated based on data from the Asian Development Bank; note that it is not weighted by population.*

Conversely, there are substantial gender gaps in educational enrollments in Sub-Saharan Africa that increase as one moves up the educational hierarchy. The share of vulnerable employment is much higher in Sub-Saharan Africa than in South-East Asia, for both women and men (83.9 percent for women and 71.3 percent for men), with women's informal and household work responsible for much of the region's food production. These aggregate figures, though suggestive, do not adequately convey the complexity of women and economic development in Sub-Saharan Africa, however, as women are at once essential economic producers and lack a number of the fundamental rights and privileges typically afforded to those with so much responsibility for the family's well-being. For instance, women's property rights, especially once married, are weak to non-existent in many Sub-Saharan African countries, and even where property rights do exist, they are often not enforced in traditional communities outside of urban centers (Joireman 2008). These types of gender inequalities have been at the heart of much of the work on obstacles to agricultural productivity in the region, as we discuss below in the section on gender equality and economic growth. Macro circumstances such as its colonial history, ongoing wars and political strife, and the extensive human costs of the HIV/AIDS crisis must be considered as well, as goals of gender equality are substantially hampered by the economic circumstances upon which they are drawn.

A similar point can be made with regard to Latin America and the Caribbean, where decades of financial crises, their associated debt burdens and the structural adjustment policies applied in exchange for debt restructuring by the World Bank and the International Monetary Fund have drawn women increasingly into the labor force in a region where female labor force participation has been historically low. This is one of the reasons why the female unemployment rate is

so high relative to the employment rate. The vast majority of women's employment is in the services sector, about 75 percent in 2008. Latin America and the Caribbean also have the lowest rates of vulnerable employment in the developing world (a 31.5 percent share of all employment for women and a 32.1 percent share for men), and the share of women in wage employment in the non-agricultural sector is on a par with developed regions at 22.2 percent in 2009. These laudable figures contrast with reports that the informalization of employment is on the rise in the region, so the ILO's vulnerable employment data should not be taken at face value (ELAC 2010). Education has been an important area of success for the region. Women have achieved parity with men in enrollment in primary school, and surpassed men in secondary and tertiary enrollments. Despite these aggregate improvements, the increasing incidence of single female household headship, and the poor economic terms upon which women entered the labor force in recent decades are ongoing obstacles to making paid work translate into gender equality (ECLAC 2010).

Middle East and North Africa (MENA) and South Asia (SA) are sometimes grouped together as the regions with the poorest records on integrating women in economic development, as evidenced by a number of indices such as the GEM (figure 8) and the GGG (figure 9). Female labor force participation rates are extremely low. The female adult employment to population ratio in 2008 was 37.7 percent for South Asia, 24.0 percent for the Middle East, and 26.3 percent for North Africa (compared to 86.7 percent, 81.6 percent and 81.7 percent for men respectively). Female unemployment rates are extremely high in the MENA region, both absolutely and relative to men (about 15 percent compared to about 8 percent for men in 2008), and much lower with less gender disparity in South Asia (6.0 percent for women and 5.1 percent for men). The structure of employment is also quite different in the two regions, with vulnerable employment in the agricultural sector representing the vast majority of income-generating employment for women in South Asia, with services the majority sector in the MENA region. In terms of education, North Africa has achieved near parity between men's and women's enrollment rates, with women's enrollment outpacing men's in tertiary education. The Middle East has done less well, with women lagging behind men particularly in terms of secondary education enrollment rates. Outside of primary school, gender equality in education is lowest in the South Asian region, with 2007 female-to-male enrollment ratios of 85 in secondary education and 77 in tertiary education. It seems that in South Asia, women still face a lot of discrimination in education and employment, while in the MENA region, the gender gap in education has declined, but there are still problems for women in the employment sphere (Klasen and Lamanna 2009).

CHAPTER 4 AN ANALYTICAL FRAMEWORK FOR GENDER AND ECONOMIC DEVELOPMENT: MICRO-MESO-MACRO

The purpose of this section is to provide an analytical framework that serves three functions: (1) To illustrate the gendered nature of the micro-, meso- and macro-levels of the economy; (2) To show how standard economic approaches to development can be improved by incorporating a gender-aware perspective; and (3) To provide an analytical foundation for assessing the policy applications in the remainder of the report.

This framework draws heavily from the work of Diane Elson, an early and frequent proponent of the argument that gender extends beyond the realm of female and male at microeconomic level into the higher order aggregates of the economy (Elson 1995; 1997; 1998). Saying that the economy is gendered does not mean that there are males and females, but that the "modes of operation" of the economy are structured by the prevailing gender order (Elson 1998: 197). In other words, the economy is not intrinsically gendered, but it is a "bearer of gender" in the sense of being structured by institutions and systems of advantage and disadvantage that themselves are gendered (Elson 1994).

4.1 Bargaining and Autonomy in the Household

It is at the micro-level, represented by the individual or the household, that most development economists situate gender issues and interventions. This is perhaps even more true now than it was ten or twenty years ago, as the increasing popularity of using random experiments to study poverty has led to a sort of "microfundamentalsim" in development

economics (Rodrik and Rosenweig 2009). To draw out the gendered nature and implications of the economy at the micro-level, in this section we develop a conceptual intra-household bargaining model that illustrates how gender shapes an individual's opportunities, constraints, priorities, needs, voice, achievements and empowerment – all in the context of a household that functions in a spirit of both cooperation and conflict.[8]

4.1.1 Choices and Constraints

In thinking about how gender shapes economic life at the household level, it is important to situate the choices of women and men within a social and material context. These contexts can be usefully categorized into what economist Nancy Folbre (1994) terms "the structures of constraint": the preferences, norms, assets and rules that shape individual choice.

Beginning with preferences, individuals make decisions about their economic lives, a process sometimes referred to as exercising agency or, in the language of utilitarian economics, "desire fulfillment." But self-perception, what individuals value, and what choices they perceive as possible are constituted by the social world, and so the putative preferences that underlie an individual's objectives must be understood in this light (Sen 1990). For instance, the objectives that drive women into the labor market can be different from those governing men, with different implications for the price of labor.

---

8 This section draws on Braunstein (2006).

Women who expect to leave the labor force for full-time motherhood may prefer the structure of easy-access, high-turnover jobs that give them a chance to live away from home and exercise freedoms they would not otherwise be able to enjoy.

Norms are the traditional structures of gender and kinship that constitute the meaning and social expectations of women and men in the household. They typically change throughout the course of an individual's or household's life cycle. Perhaps the most salient factor here - one that underlies many of the other household-level constraints we discuss - is the sexual division of labor. Women are primarily associated with the care and reproduction of the family, and much of their work time is spent outside of the market, whereas men's work is typically viewed as more directly productive and more fully incorporated into the market sphere.

Household assets, or wealth, structure household production in two distinctive ways:(1) the combined assets of all household members determine the extent of income-generating activities the household requires to meet its consumption needs; and (2) an individual's own assets help determine their influence over household decisions. In a bargaining framework like the one presented below, an individual's own wealth (in the form of land, housing, financial savings, etc.) can have different effects on household decisions than wealth controlled by others in the household.

In terms of rules, property rights and family law are crucial determinants of the relationship between women's economic decisions and their empowerment because male authority in the household can be buttressed by law. Patriarchal property rights, where eldest men have the right to claim and apportion the fruits of all household members' labor time, can create incentives for high fertility and lower female labor force participation

(Braunstein and Folbre 2001). Not having a legal claim on a spouse's income in the event of separation means that a paying job can be an insurance policy against loss of that support (Folbre 1997).

In the next section, we will develop a bargaining framework that illustrates the various ways these structures of constraint condition the relationship between a household's economic decisions and the well-being, autonomy and empowerment of its constituent members.

4.1.2 An Intra-Household Bargaining Model

The organizing principle behind the model is that individuals live in households where one's input into resource allocation and distribution decisions depends on one's alternatives to remaining in the household (exit) and one's right or ability to try and influence household decisions (voice or autonomy), including decisions about one's own strategic life choices.[9]Figure 12 illustrates the flows of the model. Starting at the top with the bargaining dyad, denoted by the symbols for male and female but representative of any combination of household members (e.g. a parent and child), both individuals begin with a set of priorities and needs. These roughly correspond to what economists typically refer to as a person's objective or utility function, and include all of a person's desires and responsibilities in the context of household production and one's role in that production.[10] Priorities and needs are fulfilled by market and non-market goods and services, including services produced exclusively by time such as childcare. (Note that in this discussion, non-market refers to both the absence of a monetary exchange, as when goods or services are exchanged among household members, and to movements of money outside the market mechanism, e.g.

---

9 This system of voice and exit reflects points made in Katz (1997), based in turn on the work of economist Albert O. Hirschman.

10 However, the standard rational actor model, and the utility functions associated with it, typically presume only economically self-interested behavior.

donations or public transfers.) Priorities and needs also tend to be gender specific in that there is likely to be a gender-based division of financial or household responsibilities, which in turn are determined by factors such as social norms or stage in the life cycle.

In order to fulfill priorities and needs, each person acts on a set of constraints and opportunities. These include time, market wages, prices, non-wage income, the probability of getting paid employment, and nonmarket transfers of goods and services like public housing or time from kin and community. Time captures the notion of labor inputs, and as such overall health and well-being are an essential part of the bargaining problem. The combined set of individual constraints, and priorities and needs, establish an individual's "provisioning capacity." Provisioning capacity thus captures each person's ability to fulfill their own wants and needs, as well as the responsibilities they have to others.

Households are taken to produce in a context of cooperation and conflict. That is, they combine their capacities to provision as collective households, but in ways that reflect their common and differing priorities. This bargaining process is represented by the black rectangle in the middle of the figure. The result or outcome depends first on gains to cooperation and then ultimately on voice. Gains to cooperation are the difference between individual provisioning capacity (PC) and terms of exit (E). Exit is captured by the determinants of what happens, should cooperation break down: one's fallback position. This includes an individual's own income, which in turn is determined by wages, the probability of finding a job, unearned income, prices for the market goods included in individual provisioning capacity, and gender-specific environmental parameters (GEPs). GEPs (a term borrowed from Folbre (1997)) describe how one's gender determines options outside of cooperation, independent

of stocks of human and nonhuman capital, the rates of return on them, prices and non-wage income. Examples of GEPs include social norms and laws surrounding the distribution of the responsibilities and costs of caring for children, the extent of public transfers (as they are determined by gender), and the probability of enjoying a share of another person's income through remarriage.

Both one's provisioning capacity and terms of exit are central to intra-household bargaining power. The greater one's priorities or needs relative to one's opportunities and constraints, or the less attractive one's options outside of household cooperation, the less bargaining power one will have. From a gender perspective, these differences are clearly very significant, as women tend to have greater needs and constraints, as well as lower terms of exit, than men.

One of the main factors in this model is autonomy in decision making, as denoted by voice in figure 12. Voice is the socially-determined capability women and men have to transmit a given bargaining position into power in the family, and it ranges between zero for social norms that completely prohibit (most commonly) women from expressing themselves and their wants and needs, and one, indicating a single adult-headed household. When there is equality between men and women in the family, voice is equally weighted at 0.5 for both women and men. The bargaining process is the application of voice to the interplay of the two individuals' gains to cooperation.

Bargaining outcomes are dependent on all of the factors discussed above. These types of models typically focus on issues of household income, consumption and distribution, and how, for instance, income under women's control will have a different well-being impact than income under men's control. But they can also give significant insights into a number of different development outcomes, including

FIGURE 12: **An Intra-Household Bargaining Model**

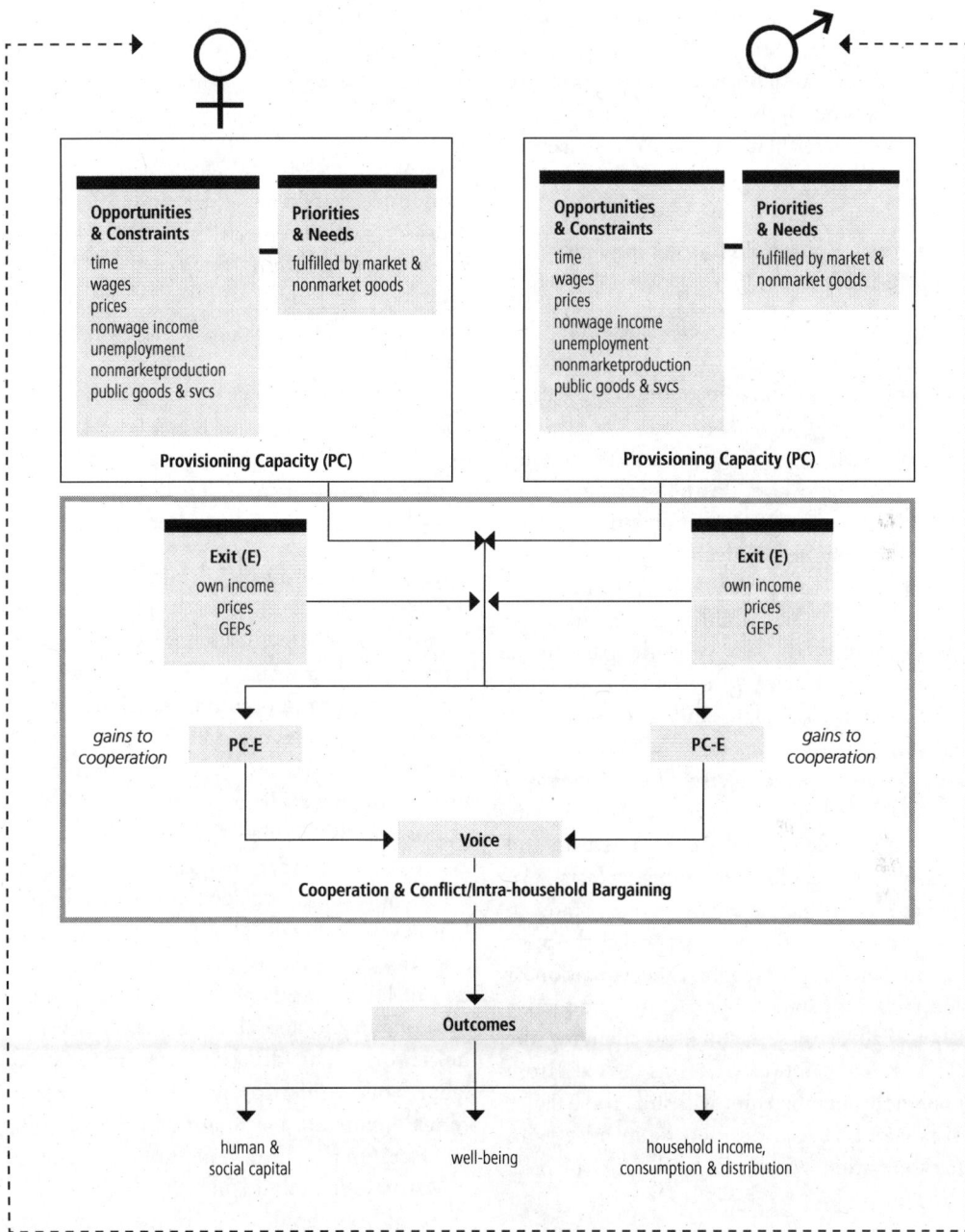

questions about the capacity of wages to increase female autonomy and the conditions under which an expansion of paid work may or may not contribute to greater health and well-being. Because outcomes feed back into the individual, and by extension the household, the entire model helps explain the dynamics of power and production in the household.

4.1.3 Intra-Household Bargaining and Gender Equality

The bargaining model specifies the parameters to consider in order to answer the question of how economic activities, such as earning outside income, contribute to gender equality and women's autonomy at the household level. In the short term, the malleable elements of an individual's power in the household are given by their gains to cooperation. These gains are captured by women's individual abilities to fulfill their provisioning needs, relative to the parameters of exit. So parameters given by time, income, prices, unemployment, and gender-specific environmental parameters, such as child support laws, are all determinants of women's and men's bargaining power. Changes in any of these parameters will yield immediate and tangible household bargaining effects. An increase in the female unemployment rate, an exchange rate devaluation that makes the price of consumer imports higher, the expansion or contraction of state supports for reproductive labor – all of these factors, by changing the gains to cooperation or terms of exit from household membership, will shift the balance of power. Likewise, an increase in male gains to cooperation will also tip the balance towards women.

The mapping of one's gains to cooperation into bargaining power is mediated, though, by voice, which is fixed in the short-term. Achieving gender equality in property rights by legal fiat, for instance, may do little in the short-run to alter the terms of exchange between women and men when social norms

prevent women from even negotiating. In the longer-term, norms do change (sometimes as the result of legal fiats), and voice becomes a variable determined by the same sorts of parameters as fallback positions.

To see how the model creates a better understanding of the relationship between economic activities and gender equality, consider what the model indicates about the importance of earning one's own income. In extremely patriarchal societies where women have no voice, working for a wage contributes only to family income and purchases as controlled by the male household head. As one moves more towards a gender egalitarian distribution of voice, women's ability to translate earned income into having a say in household decisions is enhanced.

In the longer-term, earning one's own income may in and of itself enhance voice. In societies where social norms afford men more voice than women, the effect of women entering paid work on intra-household gender relations depends on the extent to which this work challenges traditional sources of patriarchal power. In economies where social norms inhibit women from exercising their exit options, gender inequalities will persist in the household and society at large, despite high levels of female labor force participation. For instance, forms of employment that do little to challenge traditional gender relations in the household, such as industrial homework, may draw women into market labor while conferring few of the benefits in terms of enhanced autonomy (Kabeer 2000). In fact, men's intra-household bargaining power could result in men getting a greater share of household resources than what they bring into the household, suggesting that households headed by women alone could be better off than their married counterparts (Folbre 1991).

4.1.4 Autonomy and Empowerment

This section addresses the difference between the notion of autonomy as it is used in the bargaining model, and the idea of "empowerment." The difference between the two is important because empowerment is a central feature in the discourse on development, and the connection between autonomy and empowerment is not immediately clear.

My definition of empowerment is drawn from Kabeer (1999) and entails "the processes by which those who have been denied the ability to make choices acquire such ability" (Kabeer 1999: 437). She proposes three dimensions to empowerment: resources, which are pre-conditions; agency, which is a process whereby individuals define their goals and act upon them; and achievements, which are the outcomes of empowerment. In the intra-household bargaining model above, the notion of opportunities constraints and exit parallel "pre-conditions" in that they encompass the resources that individuals draw on to effect decision-making power. And voice, or one's ability to exercise choice, in conjunction with one's priorities and needs, or how one defines one's goals, is akin to the notion of "agency." "Achievements" are measured in the same way for autonomy and empowerment. The key difference between autonomy and empowerment is that empowerment implies a process, and autonomy is more like a snapshot that takes agency as an outside parameter, a static version of empowerment. Making agency endogenous, and introducing dynamics into the model, can illustrate the process of empowerment.

This framework defines autonomy on an individual basis in relation to bargaining in the household, with particular reference to the conjugal relationship. Focusing on equality in the conjugal relationship is significant for achievements that fall outside the approved boundaries of women's activities, a key part of improvements in women's well-being.

This point is illustrated in a close reading of some empirical studies of women's empowerment and health by Kabeer (1999). In discussing a study by Kishor (1997) of Egyptian data that explored the effects of women's empowerment on infant survival rates and infant immunization, Kabeer noted that women's education and employment, as well as "equality in marriage," all had a direct influence on the likelihood of child immunization. Conversely, only women's employment affected their children's survival chances. She suggests that this is the result of childhood immunization requiring more active agency on the part of mothers than the more routine forms of health-seeking behavior that are linked with improved child survival.

While power in the conjugal relationship can be a critical component in determining the scope of choice and the extent of achievements, empowerment is a term that is used much more expansively in development practice, with direct linkages to meso- and macro-level dynamics. For instance, the United Nations Population Fund defines women's empowerment as: women's sense of self-worth; the right to have and make choices; the right to access resources and opportunities; control over women's own lives, both within and beyond the household; and the ability to influence social change national and internationally (UNDP 2008: 9). Even though autonomy and empowerment are defined in a much more limited, exclusively microeconomic way in the household model discussed in this section, meso- and macro-level factors determine autonomy and empowerment as well. For instance, gender differences in economic opportunities, community norms around age at marriage, divorce, migration, and legal rights are all determinants of gains to cooperation – the difference between an individual's provisioning capacity and terms of exit. These gender-specific dynamics underlie bargaining power in the short-term, and ultimately shape an individual's ability to bargain in a dynamic context by influencing voice, preferences and norms. In the next section we will take up these issues, drawing out both these effects and how the macro and meso are themselves structured by gender relations.

4.2 A Gender-Aware View of the Macroeconomy

Macroeconomics is the branch of economics concerned with aggregate economic flows and dynamics. Areas of focus include economic growth, inflation, unemployment, interest rates, and issues related to international trade, exchange rates and the balance of payments. A good way to understand how most macroeconomists see the economy is via the standard circular flow diagram, a mainstay of introductory economics education. Figure 13 depicts the circular flow, which illustrates the flow of goods and services and money between firms and households. Households supply labor, land and capital to firms in exchange for wages, rents and profits via factor markets. Firms supply goods and services to households in exchange for payment via product markets.

These circular flows illustrate the macroeconomic dynamics of production. When the economy is in equilibrium, aggregate demand, provided by households, is supposed to equal aggregate supply, provided by firms. How this equality between aggregate demand and supply is brought about, however, depends on the theoretical approach taken (Elson 1998). Keynesian economists argue that the economy does not automatically tend towards an equilibrium between aggregate demand and aggregate supply, and that using monetary and fiscal policies to guide the economy is essential to managing macroeconomic crisis and maintaining stable growth. Conversely, neoclassical economists believe in the self-equilibrating mechanisms of flexible prices, wages and interest rates to bring about balance between aggregate supply and demand.

One thing that both Keynesians and neoclassicals do tend to agree on, however, is that the macroeconomy is largely gender neutral. In other words, the standard topics of macroeconomic study, like inflation, economic growth, unemployment, and the markets that organize firms and households to produce

FIGURE 13: **The Circular Flow of the Macroeconomy**

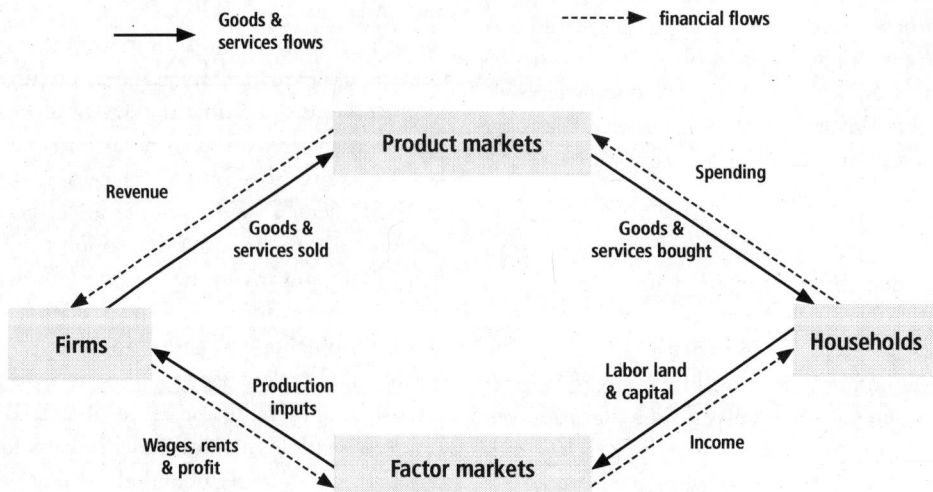

FIGURE 14: **An Alternative Circular Flow**

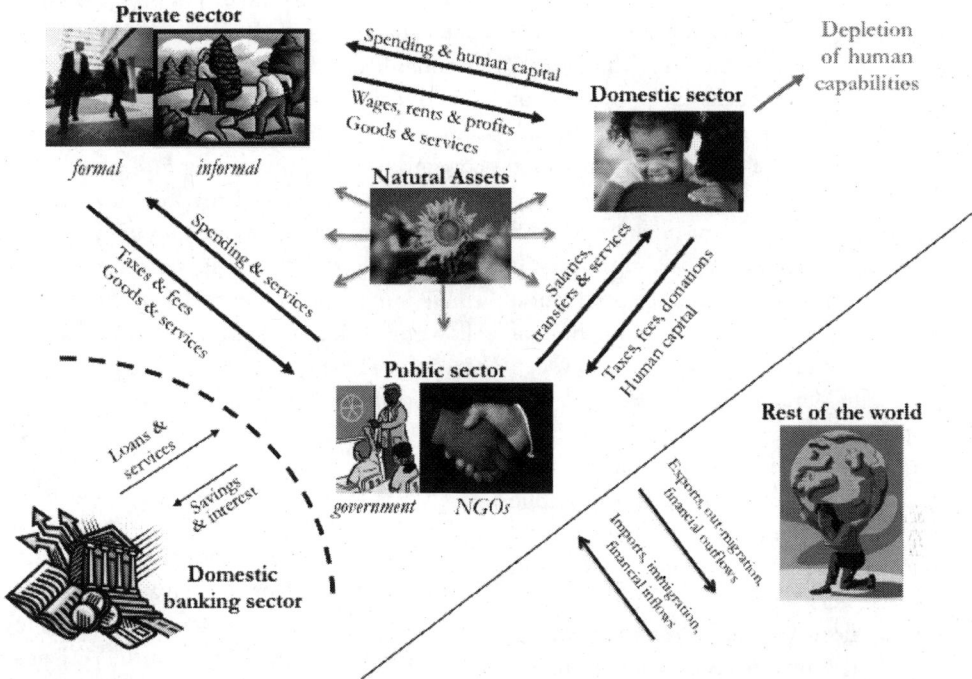

these economic aggregates, are essentially above the fray of complex social interactions like gender relations. One of the practical results of this standpoint, familiar to many GAD practitioners, is that the institutions and people tasked with macroeconomic research and management – ministries of trade, finance or growth, or their counterparts in international development organizations – defer gender concerns to other, typically less prestigious departments like labor, health, or microfinance.

Even within its own ostensibly gender-neutral rubric, however, the standard circular flow approach leaves much to be desired. It ignores human capabilities, social or natural assets – the production and maintenance of which fall primarily outside the market sphere. Labor and natural resources ebb and flow according to the market prices they fetch; the social norms, relationships and institutions that organize the functioning of markets, firms and households are completely invisible. Circular

flow approaches rarely even acknowledge the public sector, as the government is not taken as producing anything, but merely acts as a conduit for transfers from one sector of society to another (Elson 1998). The financial or banking sector is not included, partly because the role of money is merely to equilibrate macroeconomic imbalances (at least in the neoclassical model), and thus finance does not have any long-term or qualitatively significant effects on the "real" economy (i.e. the production of goods and services). Similarly, the relationship between the global economy and macroeconomic flows and balances is not part of the core circular flow model; it is an addendum that often amounts to adding exports and subtracting imports from national production figures. Once again, financial flows, this time of the international variety, are more about equilibrating prices like exchange and interest rates than a potential source of volatility that has real macroeconomic effects.

Figure 14 illustrates an amended circular flow diagram that incorporates these missing factors, forming a basis for drawing out the gendered nature of the macroeconomy. There are six sectors instead of two. The private sector corresponds to firms in figure 13, but explicitly breaks out the formal and informal sectors to underscore important variations within the private sector. The domestic sector replaces the household sector in figure 13, and includes both households and communities. It is where social reproduction, or the production of human capabilities via a combination of people and commodities, takes place. When the flow of income, goods and services, and the supply of time and natural assets are not enough to maintain social reproduction, human capabilities get depleted. The public sector includes both governmental and nongovernmental organizations. It supplies salaries, transfers like income supports, and services to the domestic sector in exchange for taxes, fees, donations and labor. A similar relationship exists between the public and private sectors, though here is added the purchase of goods and services by the public sector from the private sector.

The domestic banking sector supplies loans and services to the public, private and domestic sectors in exchange for savings and interest payments. In the center of the diagram is a representation of natural assets, with the outgoing arrows representative of how the relationship between this and the other sectors is most often a one-way flow: economic activities tend to draw on natural resource stocks without replenishing them. If or when these stocks become too low, it will constrain productivity in the other sectors. The sixth sector is termed "the rest of the world," a naming convention borrowed from international economics. Inflows to the domestic economy include imports of goods and services, people in the form of immigration, and financial inflows, including remittances. Outflows to the rest of the world include exports, out-migration, and financial outflows.

As in the standard diagram, these six sectors are linked via flows of money and goods and services, but these flows are not always mediated by markets, as is presumed in the standard approach. They are also mediated by nonmarket exchanges of money, goods and services, such as when non-governmental organizations provide reproductive health services to poor women or international migrant workers send money home to their families in the domestic sector. Sometimes there is a mix between market and nonmarket flows on various sides of the same exchange, as in cases where governments hire personnel in labor markets, paying their wages by collecting taxes from the private and domestic sectors.

To draw out the gendered nature of the circular flow mechanism, we need to look more closely at its constituent parts, what Diane Elson and others have termed meso-level institutions. Meso refers to institutions that essentially "economize on the cost of [or organize, not always in economizing ways] conducting transactions" (Elson 1994: 34). There are two sorts of meso components: (1) sectors, which refer to the six sectors of the circular flow diagram, and (2) the institutions that structure and mediate relations between sectors. The latter include markets, of course, as well as the legal rules and social norms that guide both nonmonetary and monetary relationships, including markets. These meso sectors and institutions are not intrinsically gendered, but they are bearers of gender in the sense of being structured by a society's prevailing gender order.

The structure of production in the domestic sector is perhaps the most obviously gendered, with women more likely to engage in the direct production of human capabilities than men, though men's financial contributions to this process are also important. Thus, the quantity and quality of labor supplied so often assumed in macroeconomic models of growth is an outcome of the gendered relations of reproduction. That the household is often treated as private, indeed sometimes as an individual, runs completely counter both to its role in producing human capabilities, and to the fact that family relations are themselves a product of gendered rules and norms. For this reason, Elson argues that the household or family should also be categorized as a meso-level institution (Elson 1994).

Similar gendered divisions of labor prevail in the way the natural assets sector is articulated with the wider economy. Consider the importance of forests to the livelihoods of many of the world's poor. Men and women tend to engage in different types of forest-related production, with men more involved in high value-added activities like cutting and hauling timber, and women in more traditional small scale activities, such as home gardening or collecting firewood for the household (FAO 2009). It also seems to be the case that forests are more important for rural women's livelihoods than for men's though the extent of this difference varies by locality (Ibid.) Deforestation will thus impact women and men differently, with different feedback effects on the macroeconomy.

Turning to markets, consider the overwhelmingly gendered nature of labor markets, for instance. The segregation of industries and occupations by gender across the world means that women and men experience systematic differences in unemployment as economic contractions and expansions affect some industries more than others. Speaking of a national unemployment rate masks these structural differences, and potentially mis-specifies the relationship between unemployment and other economic sectors. The fact that women typically balance their productive roles in the private and public sectors with their reproductive roles in the domestic sector means that increases in demand for women's market labor will have repercussions for the production of human capabilities in the domestic sector, with implications for current and future rates of economic growth.

In terms of rules that structure economic relationships, consider property rights, which are heavily skewed towards men in much of the developing world. In a study of farmland titles in Latin America, 70-90 percent were held exclusively by men, with similar levels of concentration among men in Sub-Saharan Africa (Deere and Leon 2001; Doss 2005; Quisumbing, Estudillo and Otsuka 2004). Though many countries have implemented legal reforms to ensure that women own and inherit land and property in their own names, there remains a marked difference between de jure (what the law says) and de facto (what happens in practice) property rights. From a macroeconomic standpoint, the possibility that land allocation and investment decisions are structured and constrained by gendered norms and rules introduces a wedge between aggregate demand and supply that neither neoclassical prices nor Keynesian demand management is designed to overcome.

The gendered pathways that run between the micro, meso, and macro (or just the meso and macro, if we treat the family as a meso institution) can go in either direction. In the remainder of this report we will explore both lines of causality, using the micro-meso-macro framework developed in this section to better understand gender and economic development, and to consider how these insights can be transformed into policy and research priorities. Sections 5 and 6 focus on the macro to micro direction, reviewing the promise of globalization to deliver employment gains and thereby enhance women's empowerment, and evaluating the impact of central bank policy on women's versus men's employment. Sections 7 and 8 illustrate the micro to macro direction, reviewing the literature on the impact of gender inequality on economic growth, and discussing the care economy from a macroeconomic perspective.

CHAPTER 5 GLOBALIZATION, LIBERALIZATION, AND WOMEN'S EMPOWERMENT

Economic globalization as it currently exists is alternately used to refer to a number of phenomena: the increasing international integration of markets and production systems; the neoliberal institutions and rules that guide that integration via a process of deregulation and privatization; and the growing exposure of national economies to external economic shocks. This section utilizes the engendered macro/meso/micro framework to illustrate how globalization affects women's empowerment at the micro level. These are important pathways to consider from the perspective of gender and development because trade and investment liberalization introduces the prospect of lessening gender inequality by increasing the demand for women's labor, particularly in developing countries. However, as discussed below, these (largely export-generated) employment effects must be considered along with the other dynamics that globalization introduces into the processes of work and provisioning.

5.1 Globalization and Women's Employment

Globalization underlies the nearly universal increase in women's share of the nonagricultural labor force among high growth developing countries in the past few decades, a result of the tremendous growth in manufacturing trade and export processing from developing countries (Barrientos, Kabeer and Hossain 2004; Standing 1989, 1999; UN 1999). The associated increase in demand for female labor is not just a matter of expanding the available labor force when male labor is in short supply. With labor costs such a crucial part of international competitiveness, labor intensive exporters prefer to hire women both because women's wages are typically lower than men's, and because employers perceive women as more productive in these types of jobs (Elson and Pearson 1981). Foreign investors looking for low-cost manufacturing platforms conform to the same pattern, at least on the lower rungs of the value-added ladder. At the same time, women may lose their comparative advantage in these job markets as industries upgrade, leading to a de-feminization of manufacturing employment as has happened in Mexico, India, Ireland and many parts of East Asia (Elson 1996; Joekes 1999; Fussell 2000; Ghosh 2007; UNRISD 2010).In terms of East Asia, there is a sense that women's manufacturing employment peaked in the mid-1990s (Ghosh 2007).

These results are consistent with recent research on multinational corporations and how they increasingly use outsourcing to break up the production value chain (a process that is more formally called "trade in intermediate inputs" in economics). It is increasingly cost effective to locate various parts of the production process in different countries. Technological advances make quality control easier, and international trade agreements lower both the direct costs of trade taxes and the indirect administrative costs of coordinating production among many different localities. Scholars argue that this is what underlies the somewhat counter-intuitive result that foreign investment and outsourcing have raised the skilled-unskilled wage gap in *both* industrialized and developing countries (Feenstra and Hanson 1997; Hanson and

Harrison 1999; Rodrik 1997). It is counter-intuitive because standard trade theory would predict a decline in the skilled-unskilled wage gap in developing economies when opening to trade and investment, as unskilled labor is their comparative advantage and trade with advanced economies is predicted to bring about specialization in low-skilled labor intensive production. The key is perspective: production at the low end of the value chain in an industrialized country that is consequently outsourced to a developing country is actually at the higher end of the value chain from the perspective of the developing country. Hence, ongoing outsourcing of intermediate inputs is likely to speed up defeminization of the manufacturing labor force in the context of export orientation to the extent that women in export sectors are confined to the least skill-intensive parts of the industry.

Subcontracting and informalization may also have a role to play in these defeminization patterns, as women doing own account work for subcontractors linked with international trade may underlie defeminization in formal manufacturing sectors. Women working in the informal sector are under-counted in official employment statistics (Carr, Chen, and Tate 2000). Even though it is difficult to precisely characterize or quantify the informal sector, many argue that informal employment has been on the rise in developing countries, and that globalization has something to do with it (Benería 2001b; Bacchetta, Ernst and Bustamente 2009; Ghosh 2007). The extreme competitiveness of globally-integrated markets drives manufacturers to seek ever more cost savings and flexibility, and subcontracting production to smaller, more marginal firms or workers' homes is a common strategy for coping with these markets. As suggested by the ILO's data on vulnerable employment in figure 3, and the limited number of country-level studies that do exist, women are more likely than men to work in the informal sector (with the exception of North Africa), partly

because it is easier to combine informal or home work with their family responsibilities (UNRISD 2005). But firms also take advantage of this situation by structuring international production in a way that exploits women's dual roles (Ghosh 2007).

Even if informalization is on the rise in many developing countries, it is still the case that globalization and trade are associated with (formal and informal) employment expansion (Bacchetta, Ernst and Bustamante 2009). For the purposes of this discussion, we take the positive association between trade and investment liberalization and women's employment as a given, and work from the presumption that globalization is associated with increases in the demand for female labor. Whether that increased demand comes from the formal or informal sectors is, however, essential to determining the relationship between earning income and empowerment.

5.2 Supply and Demand of Social Protection and Women's Empowerment

The intra-household bargaining model of women's autonomy in section 3 suggests two liberalization effects at the microeconomic level: the wage/employment effect, and the social protection effect. Social protection as it is used here is a general term that refers to any externally-generated resources or institutions that boost women's bargaining power or autonomy in the household, including legal measures such as anti-discrimination or equal inheritance laws, or provisions that support women in their reproductive responsibilities, such as childcare services, healthcare, sanitation, clean drinking water or fuel supplies. This definition of social protection is somewhat different from the one used by the International Labour Organization and others to refer to social safety nets that focus more narrowly on countering risk in the labor market or providing social assistance to the poor. Our definition of social protection includes anything that strengthens women's provisioning capacities, fallback positions, and ultimately, via changes in social norms, empowerment.

Direct supports, such as the provision of reproductive health services, childcare services, or increases in the minimum wage all may affect women's power in the household. In addition, governments and communities can provide more indirect supports for women to enhance their negotiating capacities and boost their self-confidence via neighborhood support groups or job training. Whether one refers to social protections that support the translation of wage work into greater autonomy, or those that more directly address women's health and well-being, both types are essentially about the "enabling conditions" of empowerment provided by the community and the state. But while the social protection effect plays out in the household by constraining or enhancing bargaining power and ultimately voice, the provision of social protections happens at the level of the community and the state. This is the starting point for the model developed next.[11]

The model uses as its framework the basic idea that as trade and investment liberalization increase, two opposing tendencies will operate on the policy structures of domestic economies. On the one hand, there will be pressures toward a race to the bottom – pressures for cutting or restraining the role of the government and firms in supplying the social protections of the welfare state. Trade liberalization means cutting trade tariffs, with direct and potentially significant consequences for developing country government budgets, for which trade taxes can be a significant source of revenue. Investment liberalization (both in terms of long and short-term flows) means that government budgets are beholden to global financial markets.

Global financial markets can constrain government spending via the specter of financial outflows and crisis should that spending result in budget deficits that global financial markets or international financial institutions deem unsustainable. Some of these budget constraints result from prior financial crises and current debt servicing; others are due to conditionalities imposed by international financial institutions like the International Monetary Fund. In exchange for aid and loans, developing country governments restructure their economies via marketization and privatization, and cut government spending, despite the persistently high demands of debt servicing to pay for prior crises. In an empirical study of these issues, Rao (1999) shows that trade and financial liberalization are indeed positively correlated with what is termed the degree of liberalization-related "fiscal squeeze" – changes in the growth of trade taxes and interest expenses as a proportion of GDP.

Firms have a role to play in the supply of social protections as well. Although firms may contribute relatively little to tax revenue in developing countries (Barnett and Grown 2004), a number of social protections are delivered through employment, such as minimum wages, maternity leave, and occupational health and safety. Trade and investment liberalization enhance exit options available to firms because it is easier for them to move abroad in search of lower production costs. Liberalization also increases the international competition facing domestic firms from transnational corporations and imports, making the informalization of work an increasingly essential component of creating and maintaining global competitiveness. As such, liberalization may also contribute to a race-to-the-bottom by suppressing the ability or willingness of firms to be a conduit for social protections, even if they do not finance the protections themselves. Furthermore, part of the logic behind decreasing trade taxes is that they will increase incomes and change

---

11 This model is based on Braunstein and Epstein (1999) and Braunstein (2006), and informed by Rodrik (1997).

the structure of the economy, resulting in greater tax revenues from the domestic private sector. Liberalization makes it more difficult for governments to shift their tax structures in these ways, as firms can threaten to leave or avoid taxation by shifting production to the informal sector.

On the demand side, trade and investment liberalization may bring increases in the demand for social protections. Globalization creates losers as well as winners, and may generate more insecurity by accelerating the pace of change (Rodrik 1997). The most recent financial crisis is an unfortunately telling example of the increased exposure to external economic shocks and the resultant volatility of livelihoods that come with globalization. In recognition of the increased economic risk that globalization brings, a plethora of new social protection schemes have been proposed by national and international institutions (e.g. the World Bank's Social

Risk Management framework) as part of the post-Washington consensus, which tries to combine marketization with social protections and poverty reduction (Chhachhi 2009; Razavi 2005).

From a gender and development perspective, liberalization may contribute to increases in women's needs for social services as factors like desire for fewer children and greater sexual activity pursuant to urban or extra-household employment for young women may accompany the take-up of paid work. Trade liberalization and increasing integration within the global economy widen the scope of the cash economy, requiring women to earn money to meet their traditional household responsibilities. Expanding marketization and commodification may add to women's double burden in that they must take on two jobs – paid and unpaid – to provision their families (Pearson 2004). Traditional sources of subsistence, such as a household garden,

FIGURE 15: **Demand and Supply of Social Protection**

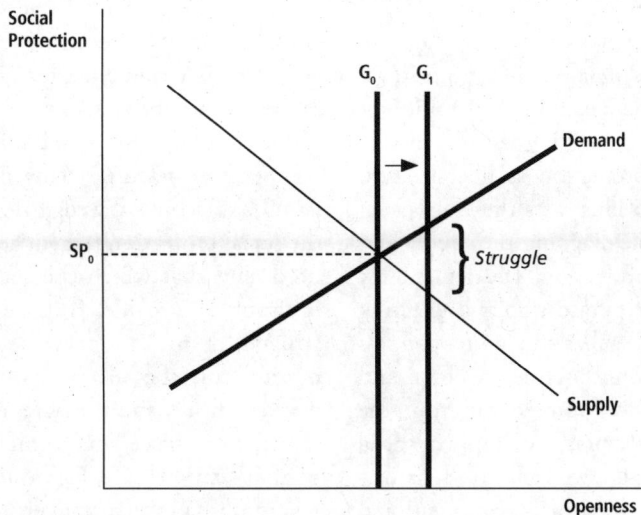

Demand: Demand for social protections by workers and citizens from firms and the state

Supply: Supply of social protection from the state and firms to citizens

G: Level of globalization

FIGURE 16: **The Effects of Liberalization on Social Protections**

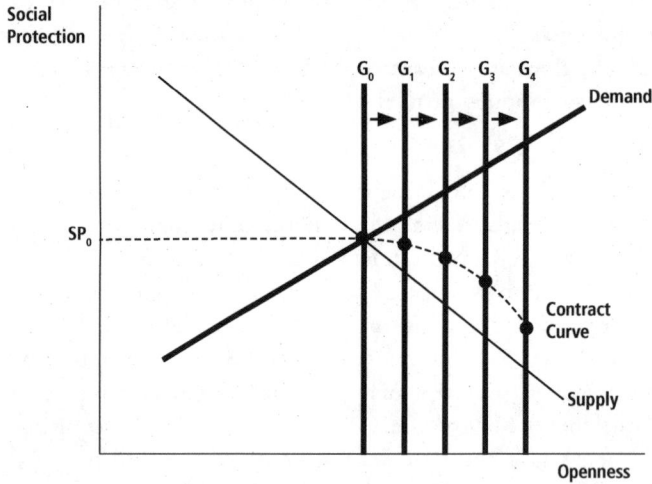

are less tenable when families move to urban centers in search of trade-related work. Also, to pursue new opportunities offered by liberalization, children must be educated and in good health. All of these factors combine to increase the support that women and families need from the community and state to carry out their provisioning responsibilities.

These conflicting pressures can operate simultaneously: the demand for more social protection, and the declining capability of the public sector or willingness of private capital to supply protection as liberalization increases. Figure 15 illustrates these opposing dynamics in a simple diagram, the supply and demand for social protection. The demand for social protection is upward sloping, reflecting the fact that as liberalization and openness to the global economy increase, women and men need more social protection from the private and public sectors. The supply of social protection represents two related dynamics that depend on the level of development and economic structure: the decreasing ability of the state to provide social supports, and firms' willingness to support social protection, either through paying taxes to government,

providing it directly to their own employees, or tolerating legislation that strengthens citizens' abilities to demand greater social protections.

The vertical line G represents the exogenously given level of globalization. A shift out in G represents an exogenous increase in the level of globalization. Such a shift may be the result of a new trade or investment liberalization agreement, which lowers government revenue (and strains government budgets), or opens the domestic market to greater import competition (and increases the competitive pressures facing domestic firms). As G shifts out, a wedge develops between the social protection that citizens and workers need, and that which the state or firms can or want to provide. This sets up a power struggle for institutional change. The outcome depends on the relative power of citizens, workers, firms, and the state, the institutional structures in place, and significantly, the level of globalization itself. Figure 16 illustrates this relationship in the current era of globalization, where greater liberalization results in increased bargaining power for private firms, both domestic and international, and weaker social provisioning capabilities on the part of the public sector. The outcome is illustrated by the "contract curve," which represents the locus of social bargains settled on as liberalization increases. Even though the demand for social bargains is actually increasing, the final outcome – where the contract curve intersects the vertical globalization line – ends up closer to the preferences of suppliers and far below public need.

The supply of social protection may be upward sloping. Through agglomeration effects and economies of scale, more openness may be associated with greater demands for infrastructure, education, and high performance work structures on the part of firms (Milberg 1998).By generating this sort of climb to the top, these effects may moderate or even eliminate the negative impacts of liberalization. But as long as the need for social protection increases at a faster rate than the supply (that is, the demand curve is steeper than the supply curve), the same dilemma, though quantitatively smaller, will still exist.

To the extent that trade and investment liberalization exert downward pressure on the supply of social protections, it lessens the capacity of the community and state, and the willingness of firms, to provide the social welfare supports necessary for women to translate employment opportunities into greater autonomy. Social services supplied by the state or community are an essential part of social protections. They constitute both an input into and an outcome of women's autonomy, and ultimately women's empowerment. Tighter government budgets and lower spending will have direct effects on women's health and well-being. These pressures also make governments less capable of using social services as a tool of women's empowerment. For instance, lower social spending on healthcare, either as a result of lower government tax revenue or cuts in job benefits offered by firms, will lower women's fallback positions. This is because where women work for pay, and bear continued

responsibility for the health and welfare of their families, their ability to assert themselves in the household is dampened by their continued need for access to male income. Furthermore, because women's employment gains are happening in sectors that are the most exposed to international competition (i.e. increases in demand for female workers coming from tradable and/or informal sectors), and increasingly characterized by informal employment relations, the bargaining power of employers vis-à-vis workers will be higher in female-dominated industries relative to other economic sectors. As a result, women are less likely to access job benefits than their male counterparts, and their intra-household bargaining power is concomitantly lower.

5.3 Making Globalization Work for Women's Empowerment

The relationship between globalization, as it is currently practiced, women's employment, and empowerment is decidedly mixed. The positive effects of increases in the demand for female labor as export sectors expand are dampened by the extreme competitiveness of global product markets and the international mobility of production and investment. Global competition and capital mobility act as brakes on wage growth even when women's employment increases, as well as contribute to the informalization of employment. The persistence of labor market segregation by gender limits women's alternatives to the most labor-intensive sectors where competition is based on cost (as opposed to quality or technological innovation), and improvements in value-added are often accompanied by declines in the demand for female labor.

Globalization has also contributed to more economic volatility for individuals and communities regardless of gender; economies are more exposed to external economic shocks and more likely to experience sudden reversals in capital flows or aggregate demand. At the same time, governments are less able, and globalized firms less willing, to provide the sorts of social protections that could counterbalance the negative effects of economic volatility and employment informalization. Evaluating these dynamics from the perspective of gender and economic development provides a sort of roadmap for finding solutions to these problems.

5.3.1 Labor Market Norms and Human Capital

At the meso-level of the labor market, breaking down the structures of gender segregation and enhancing women's human capital would afford women access to better jobs. On the supply side, as discussed at length in the household model, women's dual roles in production and reproduction need to be incorporated in policies designed to better women's employment through education and training. On the demand side, it is more about the persistence of gender norms and how employers think of work as "women's work" versus "men's work." A number of UN-sponsored projects try to address these issues, for example by providing incentives to promote women in the information technology industry in Ghana, or giving official recognition to private sector employers that commit to promoting workplace equality, as with the Equality Seal in Central America (UNDP 2008). These sorts of policies need to become a regular feature of national labor policies.

5.3.2 Localizing Firms and Increasing Women's Entrepreneurship

Strengthening locally-owned firms with strong community ties, firms that also promote women's participation and entrepreneurship, will lower some of the volatility and insecurity embedded in the contingent employment relations introduced by globalization. Firms that are integrated with *both* local and global markets, while embedded in the community, have strong incentives to increase productivity

and compete based on quality rather than price.

Microfinancing for women entrepreneurs is an increasingly popular component of gender-aware programs to alleviate poverty and should be considered in this context. In a recent review of the literature on microfinance, Naila Kabeer characterizes the results on women and microfinance as contested (UNDESA 2009). Studies of microfinance have found a number of positive effects, including increases in women's decision-making power and assets, less domestic violence, smaller gaps in girls' versus boys' education, and access to new social networks (Ibid.: 61). Other studies are more equivocal, finding that microfinance programs can at times increase domestic conflict and violence, may result in husbands simply appropriating the funds, increase indebtedness, induce too much supply in women's commodity markets, increase women's workloads, and may even lower financial contributions to households from men (Ibid.). From a macro-development perspective, there is even less consensus as to whether microfinance fundamentally challenges or changes the conditions of women's poverty and contributes to economic growth.

Applying microfinance and microenterprise principles to improving globally-oriented income-generating opportunities for women offers perhaps another avenue for women's entrepreneurship that can counter some of these more mixed results. If women-owned businesses are to serve as a real alternative to export-oriented employment, and seriously compete in the globalized marketplace in ways that ultimately contribute to development, supports for women's entrepreneurship will have to be "scaled up" and approached as more than a short-term poverty-alleviation strategy. This road will have to be explored with caution, however. As businesses get bigger and financial services more commercialized, women's representation among owners and borrowers tends to fall precipitously (UNDESA 2009).

5.3.3 Social Protections

Social policy, like economic policy, is inherently gendered (Razavi and Hassim 2006). Improving systems of social protection from a gender-aware perspective is essential, both in terms of coverage and structure. Financing is commonly seen as the limiting factor for strengthening social protections in developing countries, an issue that has spawned a lot of creative thinking and research on structuring tax systems and development aid around the provision of social protections, some of it from a gender perspective (Barrientos 2010; Grown and Valodia 2010). One of the key components to improving social protections for women is to ensure that they address women's vulnerabilities and risks in ways that strengthen women's empowerment in a fundamental and sustainable manner. For instance, when social protections such as unemployment insurance or wage subsidies are provided based on formal sector employment, women doing unpaid or informal work do not benefit. (This issue touches on what is termed "male breadwinner bias," discussed more at length in the next section.) Other types of entitlements that seem more directly geared towards women, such as measures to improve child and maternal health or old age pensions are often small and tailored to a particular stage in the life cycle, and/or designed to shore up women's roles as family managers rather than strengthen empowerment (Chhachhi 2009). Ensuring that women have a voice in decision-making processes around social protection would be an important step to improving the effectiveness of these and other public policies (Elson 2005). An example of one such effort is the Protocol on Gender and Development, which was signed in 2008 by heads of state from 12 countries attending the Southern Africa Development Community Summit in Johannesburg (UNDP 2008: 88). The Protocol commits signatories to ensuring 50 percent representation of women at all levels of government by 2015 (Ibid.).

5.4.4 International and Macroeconomic Policies

At the international level, the rules of global trade and finance as written and administered by international institutions such as the World Trade Organization and the International Monetary Fund, and a host of regional and bilateral trade and investment agreements, severely limit the ability of national governments to counter the bargaining power of multinational firms and investors, or to make public investment decisions that are good for development rather than good for global financiers. And though global policy dialogues about questions such as capital controls and national treatment may seem too far removed from the immediacy of building up women's economic empowerment, especially at the micro-level, these rules of the game pose a limiting constraint on the potential for globalization to ultimately deliver long-term gains for women.

Along similar lines, maintaining an expansionary macroeconomic environment, one where robust aggregate demand, both nationally and internationally, lowers un- and under-employment, undercuts the ability of firms to threaten to leave when wages or labor market policies are not to their liking.[12] These sorts of macroeconomic policies are sometimes referred to as "full employment" policies, though the notion of full employment – where everyone who wants paid work can find a job at a living wage – is seldom spoken of with women's unpaid work responsibilities in mind (Seguino and Grown 2006). As discussed elsewhere in this report, neoliberal macroeconomic policy tends to create sluggish economic growth and stagnant incomes for the poor and lower-skilled.

---

12 An extensive discussion of macroeconomic policy from a gender equity perspective is presented in Seguino and Grown (2006).

While raising rates of economic growth would be an improvement over current conditions, it is not enough to ensure development and the enhancement of human capabilities, especially for women. An expansionary macroeconomic environment, full employment policies, and re-envisioning the global rules of trade and financial flows must fully reflect the (gendered) social relations of production to further gender equality and women's empowerment.

CHAPTER 6   THE GENDERED TERRAIN OF CENTRAL BANK POLICY

The dominant policy position of central banks in most developing countries world wide is to maintain very low rates of inflation, without much consideration for how these restrictive policies impact the real economy – outcomes like employment, investment and economic growth (Epstein 2003). There is scant evidence that maintaining very low rates of inflation raises economic growth. Nevertheless, these policies remain a key feature of neoliberal approaches to monetary development policy (Epstein 2000). The ever increasing financialization of the global economy contributes to this stance, as central banks feel pressure to maintain an attractive investment environment (one characterized by very low inflation and high interest rates), lest they run into balance of payments problems. The result has been what many term the "deflationary bias" of the global economy, where the policies deemed necessary to mollify highly mobile financial capital results in sluggish economic growth. It might seem surprising to suggest that these types of highly aggregate financial sector policies have gender-biased effects. In this section, we consider this issue by looking at how the gender-disaggregated employment costs of inflation reduction in developing countries challenge the presumption that monetary policy is gender neutral.

This discussion is based on the work of Braunstein and Heintz (2008), who assess the impact of central bank policy on female versus male employment in developing countries beginning in 1970. They find that contractionary (employment-reducing) monetary policy aimed at reducing inflation tends to have a disproportionately negative effect on women's employment relative to men's. Their results also indicate that maintaining a competitive real exchange rate, a monetary policy option that essentially cheapens exports relative to imports, neutralizes the negative impact of contractionary inflation reduction on women's employment, with no clear pattern for men. On the other hand, in the few cases where inflation reduction was accompanied by employment growth, there was no distinct gender advantage in employment creation. That the costs of inflation reduction, at least in terms of employment, are inequitably distributed by gender means that monetary policy is affected by the gender order, with the result that the costs of implementing these sorts of policies are actually quite different – and potentially higher – than is generally presumed.

6.1 Gender Differences in Employment and Unemployment in Developing Countries

Why do women and men experience different employment dynamics when economies contract or expand, and does it matter what type of macroeconomic policy or event underlies these changes? In considering these differences, it is helpful to think in terms of supply-side factors and demand-side factors in the labor market (Seguino 2003). On the supply side, differences in human capital are probably the most commonly considered. However, gender-based differences in education, skill and experience are themselves rooted in workers' productive roles outside the factory door and the institutional, social and material contexts in which they live. The complexity of labor supply decisions are well-illustrated by the intra-household bargaining model of figure 12. Whether and how one participates in the paid labor force is an outcome of a collective household decision-making process, a process based on both individual characteristics like the wage one can earn, and the preferences, norms, assets, and rules that inform intra-household bargaining.

On the demand side, discrimination in hiring practices contributes to gender segregation in industries and occupations, a clear example being the positive association between exports and women's nonagricultural employment discussed above. That women are segregated into certain sectors and jobs underlies the notion of crowding, where an increased supply of female labor in certain classes of jobs or industries raises unemployment and lowers wages in those industries (Bergmann 1974). In a study of gender differentials in unemployment in the Caribbean, Seguino (2003) finds a positive correlation between the female share of the labor force and female unemployment (with no such correlation for men), suggesting that job segregation by sex has contributed to higher rates of unemployment for women.

Overt and more subtle forms of gender discrimination can result in gender differences in unemployment. In terms of direct discrimination, the male breadwinner ideal – the presumption that men should and do bear the primary financial responsibility for provisioning families – has been linked to higher unemployment for women relative to men in OECD countries (Algan and Cahuc 2004). Women get laid off first because employers presume that it is more important for men to be able to fulfill their traditional breadwinning responsibilities. The same link has been made between gender gaps in unemployment and gender-biased attitudes in general among OECD countries (Azmat, Güell and Manning 2006).

As a result of these gender differences in labor demand and supply, changes in macroeconomic structure and policy have differential effects on men's and women's work (Seguino 2003). From a macroeconomic perspective, some of the most important insights we have on the link between macroeconomic policy and women's employment in developing countries come from the feminist literature critiquing structural adjustment policies (SAPs) imposed largely in Latin America and Africa in the 1980s. Feminists argued that the interaction between gender relations and SAPs has implications both for the distribution of the costs and benefits of structural adjustment between different groups of women and men, and for the achievement of the economic objectives of the SAPs themselves (Benería and Feldman 1992; Benería and Roldan 1987; Elson 1991, 1995; Bakker 1994). Turning more specifically to issues of gender differences in employment and unemployment in the context of SAPs, Cagatay and Ozler (1995) use cross country data pooled for 1985 and 1990 to show that SAPs have led to increased feminization of the labor force via worsening income distribution and openness. These findings touch on gender differences in both labor supply and demand.

Economic downturns may affect labor supply in one of two ways, by either discouraging workers and pushing them out of the labor market completely, or by inducing households to add more workers to the labor market as protection against lower or more volatile household incomes, new labor market entrants that may or may not leave the labor force once the economy turns around. It is widely argued that the added worker effect is dominant in explanations of crisis-related increases in labor force participation in Latin America, much of it by women (Cerrutti 2000). Increasing labor force participation by women was also accompanied by an increase in the number of hours they devoted to paid work (Arriagada 1994). These supply effects underlie Cagatay and Ozler's results that the worsening income distribution associated with SAPs lead to an increase in women's share of the labor force. Such dynamics are not limited to SAPs. For example, research into the determinants of women's labor supply in post-apartheid South Africa shows that female labor force participation rises in response to growing unemployment, thereby further increasing the country's average unemployment rate (Casale 2003).

On the demand side, Cagatay and Ozler's finding that SAPs interacted with openness are positively correlated with feminization of the labor force reflects the shift away from import substitution and towards export-orientation associated with SAPs. But women's traditional industries have also been subject to contractionary effects. SAPs linked with deflationary stabilization that lowers domestic consumption can have adverse effects on women who produce traditional consumption goods (Standing 1999). In emerging economies, labor-intensive export-oriented industries that tend to employ women are more cyclically volatile than men's industries, resulting in higher overall rates of unemployment (Howes and Singh 1995). Emphasis on export-oriented industrialization has also been associated with increases in informalization as firms continue to minimize wage and nonwage costs (Standing 1999). So as female labor force participation and unemployment rose in the context of crisis and structural adjustment, the increasing dominance of informal work became a key feature of new labor markets for women (Arriagada 1994; Benería 2001b; Patnaik 2003).

Similar work was done on the gendered employment effects of the Asian financial crisis in 1997-1998. Women were typically the first to be laid off both because they worked in more cyclically volatile firms, such as small export-oriented enterprises, and because of efforts to protect the jobs of "male breadwinners" (UN

1999). In Korea, women lost jobs at twice the rate of men, despite the fact that before the crisis, their unemployment was half that of men's (UN 1999). According to a World Bank report in 2000, women constituted 75 percent of discouraged workers and 85 percent of retrenched workers in the banking and financial service sectors (Aslanbeigui and Summerfield 2000). Immediately after the crisis in Indonesia, 46 percent of the unemployed were women, although they made up only one-third of the workforce. And as more men became unemployed, the percentage of women engaged in paid and unpaid work increased (Ibid.). Similarly, in Thailand women constituted between 50 and 60 percent of the unemployed (Ibid.).

A slightly different pattern was found by Lim (2000) in the Philippines, where the post-crisis decline increased male unemployment more than female unemployment despite a rapid displacement of women from the manufacturing sector (especially in traded goods). The reason was the relative resilience of the service and trade sectors, which employ a high proportion of women. Women did, however, increase their labor force participation to deal with male unemployment, and their total work hours relative to men increased as well. Similar to the case of structural adjustment, the combination of increasing female unemployment and labor force participation is partly absorbed by increases in informalization. Women are increasingly pushed out of the formal sector and into the informal sector, and those that are new labor market entrants trying to preserve their household income are increasingly drawn into the informal sector as well (UN 1999).

In terms of the employment effects of the 2008 crisis, gender-disaggregated research is still sparse and merely suggestive. We do know that a substantial decline in export markets beginning in late 2008 lowered employment demand among developing country exporters. Compared to the first quarter of 2008, in the first quarter of 2009 world merchandise trade was down more than 30 percent (WTO 2009). Initial reports link women's and men's unemployment post-crisis with the industries in which they work, not with any discriminatory or male breadwinner bias as in the Asian financial crisis (Corner 2009; Hirway and Prabhu 2009). However, to the extent that this crisis has lasting effects on growth, the availability of credit, and foreign aid, we are likely to see a repeat of the informalization and intensification of work that followed the Asian financial crisis.

There are significant structural differences between women's and men's labor markets on both the supply and demand sides that are differently affected by macroeconomic structure and policy. The literature reviewed above on development and unemployment suggests that economic contractions often have a larger negative effect on women's employment than men's, though women tend to increase their labor force participation at the same time to protect household income, often entering the informal sector.

6.2 The Gendered Political Economy of Central Bank Policy

In terms of the economic implications of the Braunstein and Heintz finding that inflation reduction disproportionately affects women's employment, it is important to note that their study only addresses the short-run gender-specific impacts on employment. The results say little about the long-run impact of different policy responses to inflation, such as raising interest rates versus contracting the money supply. Supporters of inflation-targeting frequently acknowledge that short-run trade-offs might exist, but the long-run benefits of low inflation for growth and development are more significant. This argument is problematic when transitory policy shocks have long-run consequences for real economic variables (Fontana and Palacio-

Vera 2004). Similarly, short-term gender-specific shocks can have long-run effects for a country's human and economic development, as illustrated by the depletion of human capacities in the alternative circular flow of figure 14.

A number of empirical studies suggest that gender-based inequities in employment and unemployment have implications for long-term development. For example, this body of research shows that a positive relationship exists between gender equality (measured most commonly as educational equality) and economic growth in developing countries (Hill and King 1995; Dollar and Gatti 1999; Klasen 1999). Some of the effects are quite large: Klasen (1999), in a panel data study between 1960 and 1992, finds that had South Asia and Sub-Saharan Africa had more gender equity in education, growth would have been 0.9 percent per year faster. (More will be said about this relationship between growth and gender equality in Section 7.) Investing in girls makes for a higher productivity workforce, but higher rates of unemployment and cyclical volatility in women's jobs will discourage these types of investments at both the individual and community levels.

In a related sense, lower incomes and higher income volatility for women could lead to lower investments in human capital overall, thereby lowering long-term growth. Theory and evidence have aptly demonstrated a higher co-incidence between a mother's income and the family's basic needs than a father's income (Benería and Roldan 1987; Blumberg 1991; Chant 1991), a finding underlying what has been termed the "good mother hypothesis." Income that is controlled by women is more likely to be spent on children's health and nutrition (Dwyer and Bruce 1988; Hoddinott, Alderman, and Haddad 1998). In many countries, a large proportion of fathers provide little or no economic support for their children (Folbre 1994). But faced with cyclically higher rates of unemployment during disinflation, "good mothers" will have fewer opportunities to invest in their children, compromising future labor force quality.

Moving beyond instrumental arguments, the finding that women as a group shoulder a disproportionate share of the costs of contractionary inflation reduction introduces an important political economy question into the discussion: what do the distribution of the costs and benefits of inflation reduction indicate about the contested terrain of monetary policy? One might simply respond "not much," with an argument going something like the following. It is true that the empirical evidence indicates gender differences in labor supply and demand – the "gender orders" of the labor market – result in women's jobs being more cyclically volatile (at least on the economic downturn) than men's jobs in the economies studied. While macroeconomic policies (e.g. trying to reduce inflation by raising interest rates) and structures (e.g. export-oriented industrialization) may have gender-differentiated impacts, these impacts reflect gender dynamics in the labor market, not in the central bank. Monetary policymakers should not be tasked with addressing gender inequality; such issues are, and should properly remain, outside the purview of monetary management. Ultimately, the best thing (indeed perhaps the only thing) a central banker can do for gender equality is to keep inflation low and stable, as these policies provide the sort of macroeconomic stability essential for growth and income generation. Gender is only a matter of concern for social policy, the argument concludes.

The reach of this argument is also global in scope. Most central banks in developing countries are constrained by the reactions of international financial markets to their policy choices. This is particularly likely to be the case when capital markets have been liberalized and prudential capital controls have been eliminated. In addition, central banks in many low-income countries – including the heavily indebted poor countries (HIPC) – must still craft their policies under the auspices of IMF conditionalities. Monetary policies enshrined in 'poverty reduction strategy papers' reflect these biases (UNRISD 2010). Ironically, many of these 'post-Washington consensus' development strategies claim to have incorporated a gendered analysis into their poverty reduction program. However, this gender-sensitive analysis does not spill over into the macroeconomic realm.

A different sort of insight comes from thinking about what would happen if gender equality concerns were indeed incorporated into monetary policy. Such a shift would most likely necessitate a move away from inflation targeting as it is currently practiced and could harm those invested in a low inflation, high interest rate environment – largely finance capital. Even the most brief perusal of central bank leaders and managers around the world will show that they are largely drawn from finance and banking, a pool that is also primarily male. Taken from this standpoint, one that acknowledges how gender, class and nation shape our opinions of the appropriate or feasible reach of macroeconomic policy, resistance to seeing, much less incorporating, the social content of inflation targeting is clearly a political matter. It is not just that central bank policy has gender differentiated effects; it is also that the very structures of central banks and global financial markets and institutions, the permissible discourses on monetary policy, and the technical models used to illustrate them are themselves "bearers of gender" (Elson 1998).

Another aspect of the gendered political economy of these empirical findings is the point that if women's labor force participation keeps unit labor costs and inflation lower than it would otherwise be, then a focus on gender equality within the context of sustainable levels of inflation could require other mechanisms for price control that are more consistent with long-run growth and development.

Such a move might be resisted by those that benefit (perhaps only in the short-run) from women's more precarious employment – for example, their employers and employed men. Gender biased central bank policy may help solve the political problems introduced by neoliberal central bank policy in that gender bias concentrates the costs of these policies on a less powerful segment of society – women. Inflation targeting should be considered in terms of its social content (e.g., what are the social structures that underlie this policy) as well as its social impact (Elson and Cagatay 2000).

6.3 Gender-Sensitive Employment Targeting

A number of progressive alternatives to the current dominant policy position among central banks of maintaining very low inflation rates – to the exclusion of other policy concerns –call for supplementing inflation targeting with other types of targets. These include but are not limited to exchange rate targets, capital controls, output or employment targets, incomes policies to directly limit inflation, and targeted credit programs to encourage employment-creating (rather than inflation-generating) investments (Epstein and Yeldan 2009). All of these proposals would benefit from gender-aware construction and analysis.

Targeting employment generation alone, whether it be directly through employment targets or indirectly through exchange rate targets or credit programs, will not guarantee more gender egalitarian outcomes if they fail to take into account the gender dynamics of employment. If and where employment or other targets are used to assess central bank policy, these indicators must be disaggregated by gender. In light of the tremendous growth of informal employment in developing countries, these figures should include some measure of employment quality as well as quantity. Of course, data constraints may mean that this sort of labor force information is not available in a timely enough fashion to use in formulating and monitoring central bank policy. If indeed that is the case, it is important to research and formulate next-best options for tracking gender-specific employment effects.

From a gender and development perspective, it is important to remember that employment is not an end in and of itself. While employment has some direct human development implications (e.g. personal development, self-esteem, etc.), it is primarily a means to an end, a source of income that partly determines one's provisioning capacities and ultimately human development. So it is important to also consider human development outcomes as actual targets as well. Timely, detailed information that could serve as the basis for formulating central bank policies might be too costly to collect relative to other indicators such as employment. Still, gender-specific indicators of human development could be used to monitor the broader impact of employment or other central bank targets.

One issue here, which will be more completely discussed in section 5.4 on care work, is the often implicit assumption that the reproductive or care economy will seamlessly follow shifts in the paid economy. This is reflected in the notion that standard macroeconomic theory does not treat the labor force or human capabilities as produced. Even though we have yet to see some measure of care, paid or unpaid, regularly used as indicators of development, it would be essential to construct one for use as a human development target in the analysis of central bank policies.

CHAPTER 7 GENDER EQUALITY AND ECONOMIC GROWTH

One of the most compelling policy arguments proffered by development professionals these days is that gender inequality is bad for economic growth. The World Bank's Gender Action Plan's assertion that "Gender equality is smart economics" is a good example of this perspective (World Bank 2006). The economic logic for this argument is straightforward: excluding women from education, employment and other economic opportunities limits the pool of potential workers and innovators and robs economies of a key productive asset. Discrimination against women and gender inequality also tend to raise fertility, lower investments in the next generation of human capital, and restrict household productivity growth, all of which have been linked to lower rates of per capita income growth.

A number of empirical studies have tried to estimate just how much gender discrimination costs in terms of sacrificed growth. Estimating the growth costs of employment and education discrimination is the most common empirical methodology, primarily because of the wide availability of macro-level data on gendered employment and education gaps. The resulting estimates of sacrificed growth are substantial. For instance, Blackden and Bhanu (1998), in a study comparing Sub-Saharan Africa with East Asia, find that gender inequality in education and employment cost Sub-Saharan Africa 0.8 percentage points a year in per capita growth between 1960 and 1992; these inequalities account for up to 20 percent of the difference in growth rates between East Asia and Sub-Saharan Africa during the same period. A more recent study of the 1960-2000 period also estimated the combined growth costs of these education and employment gaps, finding that relative to East Asia, annual average growth rates in the Middle East and North Africa were 0.9 to 1.7 percentage points lower, and in South Asia 0.1 to 1.6 percentage points lower due to gender gaps in education and employment (Klasen and Lamanna 2009: 91).In a simulation exercise of the economic costs of male-female gaps among a number of Asian countries, it was estimated that gender gaps in labor force participation cost the region between $42 billion to $47 billion per year, and gender gaps in education cost $16 billion to $30 billion per year (UN-ESCAP 2007).

Empirical studies of the household aim to capture how gender discrimination limits household productivity and, by extension, macroeconomic growth. In a review of this literature for Sub-Saharan Africa, Blackden and Bhanu (1998) report on a number of these studies, and the results are compelling. For instance, in Kenya it was found that giving the same amount of agricultural inputs and education to women as that received by men would increase women's agricultural yields by more than 20 percent; if women in Zambia enjoyed the same level of capital investment in agricultural inputs (including land) as men, output could increase by up to 15 percent; and in Tanzania reducing the time burdens of women in smallholder coffee and banana grower households would increase the household's cash income by 10 percent, labor productivity by 15 percent, and capital productivity by 44 percent (Blackden and Bhanu 1998: xii).

FIGURE 17: **How Economists Look at Economic Growth**

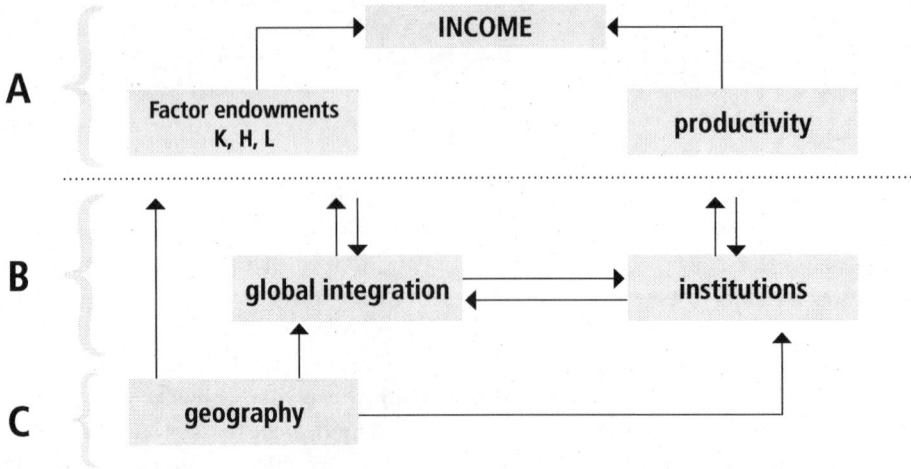

Note: This figure is based on figure 1.3 from Rodrik (2003: 5).

In this section we will critically explore how gender equality contributes to economic growth, beginning with a brief overview of how most economists think about economic growth, and the role of gender in these models.[13] We then detail the hypothesized pathways from gender equality to economic growth, covering both macroeconomic and microeconomic studies of the direct effects that gender equality has on economic growth and productivity, as well as research on the indirect mechanisms of fertility decline, investments in children, and less political corruption. We close the section with a discussion of recent research which argues that, under certain circumstances, gender inequality may actually contribute to economic growth.

7.1 Gender and Growth Theory

Open up a textbook on economic growth and you are immediately ushered into the standard core of neoclassical growth models, Robert Solow's model of long-run growth (Solow 1956). As the basis of modern neoclassical growth models, Solow's is still a pretty good representation of how most economists think about economic growth, although human capital has since been added to Solow's original model, which only included physical capital and labor supply. Solow's model is illustrated by panel A of figure 17. Panel A represents the standard neoclassical model, where income levels and growth are outcomes of two factors: (1) factor endowments and their accumulation, including physical (K) and human (H) capital, and population growth or labor supply (L); and (2) productivity. Productivity is both the main driver of long-run growth rates and exogenous to the system. Note that this growth story is confined to the supply side of the economy; there is never deficient aggregate demand, involuntary unemployment or underemployment.

13Note that in this section we focus on the impact of gender on growth, but there is also an extensive neoclassical literature that argues that growth is good for women (Dollar and Gatti 1999; Forsythe, Korzeniewicz and Durrant 2000; Tzannatos 1999; World Bank 2001; 2005).

Women have a unique place in these supply-side models, as women have long been acknowledged as a potential untapped labor supply for market growth, with little thought given to the implications of this transfer of labor for nonmarket production. A good example of this is the oft-cited work of Alwyn Young (1995), whose contribution to an ongoing debate about the relative importance of factor accumulation versus total factor productivity growth in the East Asian miracle comes down squarely on the side of accumulation – and women are a significant source of it. Changing gender roles also factor into the East Asian accumulation story via the rapid postwar decline in fertility rates in the region, which in turn lowered dependency ratios and increased savings and investment. It is estimated that this "demographic gift" contributed between 1.4 and 1.9 percentage points to East Asian per capita GDP growth between 1965 and 1990, about one-third of growth over the period (Bloom and Williamson 1997). Like changes in productivity though, rising female labor force participation and the demographic gift are largely treated as exogenous shocks, existing outside and independent of economic processes. For instance, in the case of declining fertility, which is so centrally linked to female education and employment, the causal mechanism is still presented as exogenous – a combination of declining infant mortality and the increased availability of family planning services, the results of imported health technologies and government policy (Bloom and Williamson 1997).

The fact that Solow's model lacked an explanation of its main driver – productivity growth – spurred what came to be known as "new growth theory," which models the innovation process as endogenous. Referring back to figure 17, new growth theorists see growth as a combination of panels A, B, and C, where factor endowments and productivity are themselves products of socioeconomic and natural structures and processes. Institutions

and global integration garner most of the attention in these treatments. The only truly exogenous factor is geography, which may directly affect growth via natural resource endowments such as land productivity or public health (as in the case of the prevalence of malaria). Geography also affects growth indirectly via its effects on global integration, as when a country is land-locked or endowed with significant shipping lanes, and via its effects on institutional development when the latter for instance bears the traces of colonial occupiers or the corruption often linked with an abundance of natural resources.

As indicated by the arrows in figure 17, global integration and institutions shape one another in addition to the proximate processes of factor accumulation and productivity. One can see how developmentalist states shaped global integration in the case of the so-called East Asian miracle, a type of integration that in turn partly determined the pace and structure of technical progress and factor accumulation in these countries. Of course, the seemingly spare square that represents institutions is actually a large and complicated amalgam of factors, coinciding with the meso-level sectors and institutions that appear in the amended circular flow of figure 14. However, for all intents and purposes most new growth theorists simplify this complexity in empirical work by measuring institutional quality as the rule of law and property rights (Rodrik, Subramanian and Trebbi 2004).

Income inequality is a significant aspect of this research, as lower inequality is associated with institutional quality and consequent growth (Alesina and Rodrik 1994; Perotti 1996; Persson and Tabellini 1994). The (mainstream) political economy explanation of the causal mechanisms from equality to growth is embedded in the neoclassical reasoning of markets and incentives. Perhaps the most familiar line of logic employs the median voter model to argue that higher levels of inequality result in the median voter being poor relative to a country's average income, leading to political pressure for redistributive policies and consequent reductions in incentives to accumulate physical and human capital (Aghion, Caroli and García-Penalosa 1999; Alesina and Rodrik 1994). Alternatively, imperfect capital and insurance markets inhibit the poor from making investments in physical and human capital. In such cases, redistribution from the rich to the poor can have positive net effects on output and growth (Bénabou 2000). In all of these cases, income inequality is inefficient because it lessens incentives to invest and innovate. Is the same also true of gender inequality?

The short answer is yes. Gender inequality and discrimination are inefficient because they do not maximize productive capacity. Neoclassical faith in the market mechanism anchors the theoretical basis of these approaches. Inefficiencies exist either because institutions are 'sticky' in the sense of failing to change in response to changing economic incentives, as when bankers refuse to lend to female business owners even when there are profits to be made, or because of market failures, as when the land rights system inhibits the use of land by its most productive user (Folbre 1994). The inefficiency of gender inequality in these models is not drawn in terms of power or coercion, however. Even where gender norms are resistant to change in the face of changing prices or incomes, their persistence is never really dealt with as internal to the economic system, much in the same way that early growth theory treated productivity as exogenous. As such, we are pretty much left with only the language of market imperfections to explain and alleviate gender inequality. Still, this is an interesting and important literature, a central component of the neoclassical argument that institutions matter for growth.

7.2 Direct Effects

7.2.1 Macroeconomic Studies

Macroeconomic analyses of the direct effects of gender inequality on growth focus on educational equality and the misallocation of labor. In terms of the former, the logic is that if male and female students have equal aptitudes, then educating more boys than girls will lower the overall quality of educated individuals via selection distortion effects (Klasen 1999). Alternatively, with decreasing marginal returns to education, educating more girls (who start out with lower education than boys due to gender inequality) will give higher marginal returns than educating more boys (Knowles, Lorgelly and Owen 2002; Schultz 2001; World Bank 2001). A number of studies have shown strong positive correlations between women's education and growth (Hill and King 1995; Klasen 1999, 2002; Klasen and Lamanna 2009; Knowles, Lorgelly and Owen 2002; Dollar and Gatti 1999). Similar selection-distortion effects apply to labor markets. When workers are kept out of certain occupations or industries based solely on sex, the best worker will not be matched with the most appropriate job (Esteve-Volart 2000, 2004; Tzannatos 1999). Alternatively, when women are kept out of the paid labor force completely, average labor force quality will be lower than otherwise, as more productive female workers are kept from working in favor of less productive male workers (Klasen 2005).

7.2.2 Microeconomic Studies

Microeconomic studies emphasize the inefficiencies of gender inequality as well, but the underlying theoretical models also admit the exercise of power via intra-household bargaining. Despite the admission of hierarchy and bargaining at the household level, the structure of neoclassical analysis finally limits the ability of these models to provide insight into gender. The models presume that bargaining between men and women is symmetrical; that is both have the same ability to translate a particular fallback position into bargaining power (Katz 1997). Objective functions that differ systematically by sex are taken as exogenous rather than focused on as a dynamic product of social and economic interactions. The same applies to the gendered nature of institutional structures – how things like property rights and divorce law are also themselves the result of social and economic processes. To the extent that there are inefficiencies that result from gender inequality, when they are theorized (and not just taken as a given) they are the result of market imperfections, not the result of the exercise of power itself.

Let us consider this literature to see what we mean. Limiting ourselves to work that is germane to the question of gender equality and growth, we get a variety of microeconomic approaches to the implications of imperfect property rights and capital, credit and insurance markets. Weak or nonexistent property rights for women, especially in Africa, are identified as creating production inefficiencies (Duflo 2005). For instance, in Burkina-Faso, more fertilizer is typically used on a husband's plot than on his wife's because he can afford more fertilizer. Concentrating fertilizer on the husband's plot occurs despite decreasing marginal returns to fertilizer use. Even though a more equal distribution of fertilizer between the husband's and wife's plots would raise household production, this never happens because each worker prefers a "bigger slice of a smaller pie" – the bargaining problem. Duflo argues that weak property rights prevent women from renting land to their husbands (in which case he would use more fertilizer on it and maximize production), because if the husband works the land long enough, the wife may lose her property rights. The emphasis in this story is not on self-interest or the possibilities for coercion, but about property rights and their role in the persistence of inefficiencies.

Similar issues come up in markets for capital, credit and insurance. Women have systematically weaker access to credit markets than men, partly because they command fewer resources to begin with and hence have little to offer in collateral, and partly because there is direct discrimination against women in credit markets. Particularly in agrarian or petty trader contexts, these types of credit market imperfections bar women from making production- or profit-maximizing choices. Many of the studies that deal with these issues, particularly in Sub-Saharan Africa, look at the resulting deficiencies in women's access to inputs and conclude that there are significant sacrifices in productivity that occur as a result of asymmetrical access to factors of production (Blackden and Bhanu 1999; Klasen 2005; Quisumbing 2003; Saito, Mekonnen and Spurling 1994; Udry 1996; Udry, Hoddinott, Alderman and Haddad 1995; World Bank 2001).

All of these studies soundly reject the notion that households are always harmonious and unitary sites of production. The result is that gender inequality is a significant and direct factor in the determination of productivity and output. But it is the market that is most centrally featured as both the source of inequality's persistence (imperfect/incomplete markets), and its preferred solution (realigning market incentives), a point that is central to the literature on externalities as well.

7.3 Externalities

The term externality refers to something akin to indirect effects, but with a precise relationship to the market mechanism. An externality is a sort of spin-off of an activity or transaction that affects the wider society – those who do not directly participate in the activity or transaction. Even if the prices or incentives produced by markets are well-functioning for individuals, the added social value or social cost of individual activities are not, and hence activities that generate positive externalities will tend to be undersupplied by markets relative to their social benefit, and activities that generate negative externalities will tend to be oversupplied relative to their social cost. Gender equality is argued to have a number of positive externalities for economic growth.

7.3.1 Fertility

The oldest and most well-known aspect of the gendered externalities and growth literature, one that dates back to early theories of population growth and income, is the linkage between fertility decline and higher growth. Even with constant income, lower rates of population growth will lead to higher per capita incomes. But the observed mechanism is much more complex, as briefly explained in the discussion of the demographic gift. Improvements in infant and child mortality turn into a young adult glut, spurring a savings boom and an increase in investment demand (Bloom and Williamson 1997). Fertility declines as parents turn from child quantity to quality, creating higher capital-to-labor ratios and consequent growth (Galor and Weil 1996). The corollary to this is that fertility is positively correlated with educational inequality by sex (Ahituv and Moav 2003; Klasen 1999; Lagerlöf 2003; World Bank 2001). Educating women is also documented as an important way of lowering child mortality and undernutrition, and increasing children's education, aspects of increased child quality and contributors to long-term growth (Klasen 1999; Lundberg, Pollak and Wales 1997; Thomas 1997; World Bank 2001). Lower fertility is also correlated with higher female labor force participation and gender-based wage equality (Galor and Weil 1996; World Bank 2001).[14]

The familiar logic is that as the opportunity costs (the costs of forgone opportunities) of women's time increases, parents opt for more child quality over quantity. With women doing most of the childcare, it is essential that the opportunity costs of women's time increase relative to men's, as increases in male incomes will only raise the demand for children and increase fertility.

7.3.2 Good Mothers

This point about child quality and the association between women's education and incomes and child well-being is an important aspect of the intra-household bargaining literature as well. The argument is that women are "good mothers" in the sense that income under women's control is more likely to be spent on child well-being than income under men's control (Haddad, Hoddinott and Alderman 1997; Thomas 1990), a sound rejection of unitary models of household behavior. Female influence over household consumption is of course directly linked to women's bargaining power, proxied in empirical studies by various measures such as education, assets at marriage, spheres of decision-making, divorce law, and relative status within the household and society (Quisumbing 2003). A number of studies show positive correlations between women's bargaining power and children's education and health (Murthi, Guio and Dreze 1995; Quisumbing 2003; Quisumbing and Maluccio 2003; Schultz 2001; Thomas 1997; World Bank 2001). That women invest a greater proportion of their resources in the household is perhaps not surprising, as women's spheres of influence do not often extend beyond the household (World Bank 2005). This brings up the possibility that mothers are not always altruistic, but a little self-interested like everyone else.

---

14 Fertility and female labor force participation are also likely to have mutual causation.

This perspective is reflected in Duflo's critiques of the good mother literature (Duflo 2005), though hers are largely econometric criticisms and do not challenge underlying theories of gendered preferences.

7.3.3 Corruption

The prospect of altruistic mothers touches on the positive externalities of social norms – if girls are conditioned to act benevolently towards their future children, fulfilling the role of good mother will raise investments in children and long-term growth. The positive externalities of gender norms also come up in studies of corruption and growth. Behavioral studies show that women tend to be more trustworthy and public-spirited than men, with one of the results being that higher proportions of women in government or the labor force are negatively correlated with corruption (Dollar, Fisman and Gatti 2001; Swamy, Knack, Lee and Azfar 2003). Here the logic is more about how prevailing social norms may be efficient in some ways, a process that is almost certainly at work in creating the positive externalities of good mothers as well.

7.4 When Inequality Contributes to Growth

From the perspective of the early Solow-type growth models, neoclassical institutionalists have made some headway towards making the theoretical and empirical argument that gender relations matter for growth and that there is a positive link between gender equality and economic efficiency. Market imperfections and 'sticky' institutions can lead to gender inequality, which in turn may have direct effects on growth via selection distortion-type effects in education and labor markets, and create growth-inhibiting incentives in investments in human and physical capital. Fertility decline, investments in children and decreased corruption are consequences of gender equality with positive

externalities for growth. Thus gender equality bears instrumental relevance and international institutions and development agencies have a sound empirical basis for promoting gender-aware approaches to growth and development – the efficiency argument. However, as argued in the discussion of the amended circular flow, markets and other economic institutions are themselves products of the prevailing social order, including the gender order, and can be used in ways that benefit some over others. Institutions are slow to change because individuals and societies often resist that change, at least partly because it is to their economic benefit to do so.

For instance, consider the work of economist Stephanie Seguino, who argues that gender-based wage gaps have actually contributed to growth among semi-industrialized countries (Blecker and Seguino 2002; Seguino 2000a, 2000b, 2000c, 2008). Seguino posits that the development of many economies is limited by the small size of their domestic markets (they are demand-constrained), and by a lack of foreign exchange to purchase technology-enhancing imports (balance of payments constraints). Where women are segregated into export sectors, as is common among semi-industrialized countries with labor-intensive export-oriented manufacturing sectors, lower female wages enhance competitiveness and profitability, raising investment and growth. In addition, there is a "feminization of exchange earnings" effect, where lower export sector wages and consequent competitiveness increase a country's foreign exchange earnings. This affords greater access to global markets in capital and technology, which also enhances growth.

Seguino's findings contradict the neoclassical literature's take on gender equality and growth. Furthermore, Seguino's work indicates that the *type* of inequality is what matters for growth. When gender discrimination is manifested in ways that do not compromise the overall quality of the labor force but merely lower the cost of labor for employers, systematically discriminating against women can have positive effects on growth. Gender differences in education *will* lower growth because it lowers the productivity of labor. East Asian governments in newly industrializing economies helped ensure wide access to basic education and health during the export-led boom years, as well as implemented and maintained policies to ensure high levels of household income equality (Birdsall, Ross and Sabot 1995). These are the key factors linking equality and growth within the neoclassical institutionalist paradigm. However, gendered hierarchies were also maintained via the incorporation of women into the paid labor market in ways that did not unduly challenge traditional gender norms.

In the case of Taiwan, strong patriarchal traditions and inter-generational obligations created high degrees of intra-family stratification based on gender and age, with unmarried daughters the lowest class in the family hierarchy. The early years of Taiwan's export-led boom were fueled by the entry of these women into export factories. Rather than threaten traditional family structures, paid work actually increased sexual stratification because it enabled parents to extract more from filial daughters (Greenhalgh 1985). In the 1970s when Taiwan faced labor shortages, the state-sponsored satellite factory system made industrial work more consistent with traditional female roles, enabling increases in the labor supply of wives and mothers (Hsiung 1996). Similarly, South Korea was able to maintain a competitive labor-intensive sector along with a highly paid male labor aristocracy by keeping wages in female-dominated export industries low (Amsden 1989: 204).

Thinking about these gender systems from a growth perspective is instructive, as it illustrates a case where gender inequality enabled growth-enhancing investments as well as payoffs for male labor aristocracies. It also lays bare the pitfalls of the efficiency argument. Standard appeals to "reason" and "efficiency" in neoclassical work on gender equality will hardly prove compelling when we understand that if equality means the loss of gendered advantage or economic rents, it will be resisted regardless of how seemingly socially efficient the attendant economic prescriptions appear. To the extent that we depend on the instrumental value of gender equality to further gender-aware economic policies, we will be consistently discouraged and somewhat mystified by continued resistance. This is not to say there are no benefits to instrumental arguments. That women's rights and empowerment have gotten some attention is certainly an improvement that is partly due to these types of arguments. But given that gender equality is costly to some in terms of the loss of power or economic advantage, resistance will remain ongoing, especially in cases where gender inequality is strongest and maintains advantage for the privileged.

CHAPTER 8   A MACROECONOMIC PERSPECTIVE ON DEVELOPMENT AND CARE

The United Nation's System of National Accounts (SNA) specifies global accounting standards for recording GDP and measuring economic growth. The SNA's "production boundary" for GDP includes all goods and services that enter the market, as well as just about any other activity that one could theoretically pay someone else to do. Examples of the latter include working as an unpaid worker in a family business, growing food for own consumption, making clothing, or collecting water or firewood for fuel. Though these unpaid activities are technically included in GDP figures, there is a lot of variation in the extent to which countries systematically survey and estimate them. It is far from an overstatement to say that unpaid work within the SNA production boundary tends to be undercounted in GDP, particularly in developing countries where data collection is relatively limited and expensive, and the size of the unpaid and informal sectors is large.

The one category of unpaid work that falls outside the SNA production boundary, even though one could pay someone else to do it, is unpaid care work. Unpaid care work refers both to direct care activities that involve close personal or emotional interaction with those being cared for, such as caring for a child, the elderly or the disabled, and indirect care activities that provide support for direct care, such as cleaning house or preparing a meal (Folbre 2006). Referring back to the standard macroeconomic circular flow in figure 13, it is perhaps not surprising that unpaid care work is left out of GDP as there is no notion of production or reproduction of labor in mainstream macroeconomic theory. In figure 14, unpaid care work is provided in the

domestic sector, drawing on goods and services purchased or transferred from the other sectors of the economy. Businesses, governments and non-governmental organizations are all involved in providing paid care services. Flows of remittances and labor underlie "global care chains" when women migrate to work as nannies, maids or nurses and send money home to provide for their own children (Folbre 2006). Care work, whether paid or unpaid, direct or indirect, is an essential component of maintaining the flow of human capital to the rest of the macroeconomy, and transforming the products of monetary production into human well-being.

Over the past couple of decades, care work has garnered increasing academic and policy attention, creating the emerging fields of the economics of unpaid work and the study of the "care economy," a term coined by Diane Elson. Most of this work, particularly that in the field of economic development, is microeconomically-oriented, focusing on issues like the household division of labor, subsistence production, and the substitution between nonmarket and market goods and services in households. Empirical work parallels these theoretical efforts. Examples include measuring unpaid work via small-scale time-use surveys, estimating the monetary value of unpaid household work, and linking care with the gender wage gap and gendered job segregation. Less work has been done on the macroeconomic aspects of care, particularly in a development context (an important exception being UNRISD's recent project The Political and Social Economy of Care).

8.1 Estimates of Unpaid Care Work in Developing Countries

The main instrument used for collecting data on unpaid care work is the time use survey. As with a lot of other types of economic data, advanced industrialized countries have a longer history of collecting systematic time use data on even a semi-regular basis for nationally representative samples than developing countries.[15] A number of UN agencies are involved in the creation, support and analysis of time use surveys across the developing world [e.g. UNIFEM (2005); UNRISD as reported in Budlender (2008)]. In this section we present a representative sample of these studies, discussing how much time women and men spend at work, both paid and unpaid, the value of unpaid care work, and the relative sizes of the paid and unpaid care sectors in a selection of developing countries.

In considering the data, it is important to make note of how time use surveys deal with simultaneous activities. Supervisory or on-call activities are most often largely invisible, since survey questions tend to ask respondents only about "primary activities" (Folbre 2006). Childcare is often categorized as a secondary activity because it is commonly combined with other activities such as preparing food or even working. The UNDESA's guide to producing time use statistics makes this point (UNDESA 2004), but there has been little work done on how exactly to ask the right questions in different cultural and economic contexts. One telling example from an advanced industrialized country: Australian time use surveys in 1992 and 1997 found three hours of childcare as a secondary activity for every one hour of childcare provided as a primary activity (Folbre 2006).

Table 3 combines the results of two recent reviews of nationally-representative time use studies in developing countries (with the exception of the Argentinean study which covered only Buenos Aires). Budlender (2008) reports on an analysis of time use surveys sponsored by UNRISD, reporting results for working age adults only; Charmes (2006) evaluates the few nationally representative time use surveys available for Sub-Saharan Africa, and includes children as young as six for Benin and Madagascar, and as young as 10 for South Africa and Mauritius. Both sets give population averages. That is, they report average time spent at work in a day across the entire population, so individuals who do not do any work in a particular category are included in the sample average with a score of zero. There are methodological, coverage, and a variety of other differences among the various time use surveys included in Table 3, though they seem close enough to usefully compare. Note that time use survey results were reported in both the Charmes (2006) and Budlender (2008) studies; the same time use survey, conducted by Statistics South Africa in 2000, is the basis for both sets of results, though Budlender's includes only adults. The SNA rows in Table 3 refer to the number of hours women and men spend on activities that fall within the SNA production boundary, regardless of whether the activities are paid or unpaid. Unpaid care work refers to time spent providing unpaid care, a category that is not within the SNA production boundary and therefore not included in GDP. Total work equals the addition of SNA and unpaid care work time. The columns delineate work time for women, men, and the ratio of female-to-male work time in the various categories by country.

15 See the United Nations Statistics Division website for more information on particular national time use surveys (http://unstats.un.org/unsd/demographic/sconcerns/tuse/).

The survey results reported in Table 3 show a number of common time use patterns across countries by gender. First, with the exception of Benin, men spend longer work hours engaged in SNA activities than women. The high is in India, where men work a daily average of 7.2 hours in SNA activities compared to 3.0 hours for women; and the low is in South Africa, with men working between 3.2 and 3.9 hours in SNA activities versus between 1.9 and 2.4 hours for women. Second, women spend more time in unpaid care work than men, with a high of 5.9 hours in India compared to only 0.6 hours for men, and a low of 2.9 hours in Tanzania compared to 1.3 hours for men. Third, again with the exception of Benin, most of women's work time is spent in unpaid care work. Most of men's work time is spent in SNA activities. And lastly, when we add together time spent in SNA and unpaid care work, women in all the surveys have a longer average work day than men. The female-to-male ratio of total hours worked in a day ranges from a high of 147 percent in Benin, where women work an average of 7.4 hours a day compared to 5.0 hours for men, to a low of 103 percent in Argentina/Buenos Aires, where women work an average of 7.3 hours compared to 7.0 hours for men.

How significant is unpaid care work relative to national income? A number of economists and others have tried to answer this question by assigning a monetary value to unpaid care work and then comparing it to GDP. There are two main approaches to appraising unpaid care work, output- and input-based. Output-based approaches value the products of unpaid care work using the price of close market substitutes, often subtracting the cost of raw materials to get at net value added. Statisticians seem to prefer this method because it is the same basic principle as that applied to valuing subsistence production in agriculture, and because production boundaries are clear (only those activities with market substitutes get

counted) (Ironmonger 1996; Pyatt 1993). This perceived advantage is also a weakness. Activities without close market substitutes are difficult to include, or production for which markets have not yet developed (such as paid eldercare in developing countries) are not assessed any value (Pyatt 1993). Additionally, data requirements are high, necessitating information not only about the time devoted to unpaid care work in households, but also about the use of purchased goods and services in the provision of unpaid care.

Perhaps as a result of these challenges, most studies use input-based methods, which value the labor time devoted to unpaid production using one of two options. The first is the opportunity cost method, where the going wage rate for an individual of similar characteristics is multiplied by the time devoted to unpaid care work. A key drawback of this method is that wage rates are separated from the type of output produced, so identical products are valued differently according to who produces them. Another problem is that systematic wage differentials between women and men get transferred to valuations of unpaid care work. The second input-based method uses the price of hiring a market substitute, either specialized (as in using the going wage for the variety of services provided by family members doing unpaid care work), or generalized (as in using the wage for a general housekeeper). Using the wage rate for a general substitute is sometimes cited as a second-best solution (Goldschmidt-Clermont 1993), because it provides the most conservative estimate and seems closest to the supposed first-best output methodology. Its biggest weakness seems to be the improbable assumption that the tremendous variety of tasks involved in unpaid care work could be performed by an unqualified housekeeper. But reverting to the specialist method brings with it the problem of assessing value for time when engaged in simultaneous tasks, such as looking after children while preparing the evening meal.

TABLE 3: Work Time in SNA and Unpaid Care in Various Countries by Gender

Estimates based on Budlender (2008)

	Argentina			India			Republic of Korea		
	Women	Men	Women/Men	Women	Men	Women/Men	Women	Men	Women/Men
SNA	3.0 hrs	5.6 hrs	54%	3.0 hrs	7.2 hrs	42%	3.5 hrs	6.0 hrs	58%
Unpaid Care Work	4.3 hrs	1.5 hrs	288%	5.9 hrs	0.6 hrs	983%	3.8 hrs	0.7 hrs	528%
Total work	7.3 hrs	7.0 hrs	103%	8.9 hrs	7.8 hrs	114%	7.3 hrs	6.8 hrs	108%

	Nicaragua			South Africa			Tanzania		
	Women	Men	Women/Men	Women	Men	Women/Men	Women	Men	Women/Men
SNA	2.6 hrs	6.4 hrs	41%	2.4 hrs	3.9 hrs	61%	5.1 hrs	6.0 hrs	85%
Unpaid Care Work	5.7 hrs	1.5 hrs	380%	4.1 hrs	1.5 hrs	276%	2.9 hrs	1.3 hrs	229%
Total work	8.3 hrs	7.9 hrs	105%	6.5 hrs	5.4 hrs	120%	8.0 hrs	7.2 hrs	111%

TABLE 3: **Work Time in SNA and Unpaid Care in Various Countries by Gender**

Estimates from Charmes (2006)

	Benin			South Africa		
	Women	Men	Women/Men	Women	Men	Women/Men
SNA	3.9	3.9	100%	1.9	3.2	61%
Unpaid Care Work	3.5	1.1	310%	3.8	1.3	304%
Total work	7.4	5.0	147%	5.7	4.4	129%

	Madagascar			Mauritius		
	Women	Men	Women/Men	Women	Men	Women/Men
SNA	2.9	4.8	60%	1.9	4.9	39%
Unpaid Care Work	3.7	0.8	470%	4.6	1.2	379%
Total work	6.6	5.6	118%	6.6	6.2	107%

Source: Author's calculations based on data presented in Budlender (2008) and Charmes (2006).

71

Figure 18 reproduces input-based monetary estimates of unpaid care work as a percentage of GDP from the Budlender (2008) study. Four methodologies were used, though not all methods were possible for all countries due to lack of data. The first two methods, "all earners" and "all employees," are opportunity cost methods. All earners uses the median earnings of all people engaged in market work disaggregated by sex, so the earnings used to value unpaid care time are different for women and men. All employees do the same except for leaving out the self-employed. The second two methods, "generalist" and "domestic worker," use the price of hiring a market substitute. Generalist uses the median wage paid to occupations similar to housework, whether preformed in institutions or private homes; domestic worker uses the median wage of workers working in private homes only. The results varied widely both across and within countries, as is usually the case with these types of estimates, ranging between a low of 7 percent using domestic worker wages for Argentina (where the gross

geographical product of Buenos Aires was used instead of GDP), to a high of 63 percent using all employees in India and all earners in Tanzania. The variation within countries between all earners and all employees on the one hand, and generalists and domestic workers on the other, is likely tied to the fact that women tend to dominate in the generalist and domestic worker categories, and that these are some of the lowest paid sectors of the economy (Budlender 2008).

Another way to gauge the value of unpaid care work is to consider it in relationship to the value of paid care work. Estimates of the value of unpaid care work as a percentage of the value of paid care work from Budlender (2008) are reproduced in figure 19. The value of paid care work includes the earnings of those working in paid occupations that primarily involve care work, both in the private and public sectors. For most of the countries in the study, these occupations included pre-primary and primary school teachers, except for India and the Republic of Korea, which included

FIGURE 18: **The value of unpaid care work as a percentage of GDP**

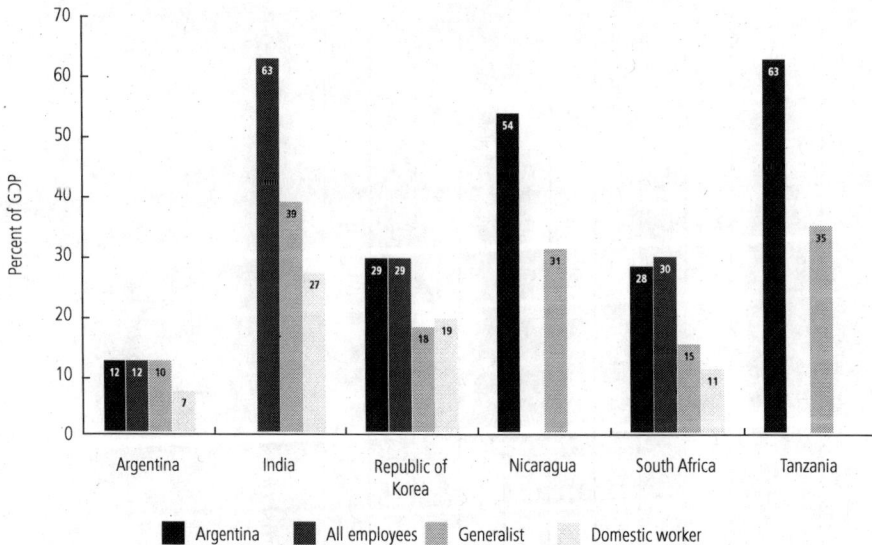

Source: Reproduced from Figure 22 in Budlender (2008: 38).

FIGURE 19: **The value of unpaid care work as a percentage of paid care work**

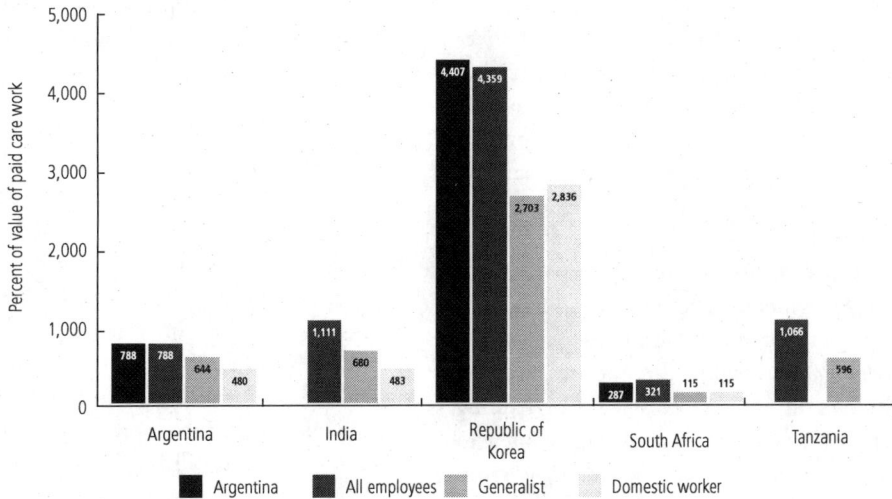

Source: Reproduced from Figure 27 in Budlender (2008: 43).

neither teachers nor any health care sector workers. This exclusion probably explains why the estimates for Republic of Korea are so high, with the value of unpaid care work ranging between 4,407 and 2,703 percent of the value of paid care work, depending on the wages used to value unpaid caring labor time. We generally anticipate that the ratio of the value of unpaid to paid care work declines as income increases, a question to which we now turn.

8.2 Economic Development and Unpaid Care Work

The conventional wisdom is that unpaid work time generally declines with economic development as the private and public sectors extend the reach of the monetary economy, and labor-saving technologies and expanded public infrastructure raise the productivity of household work. Some recent empirical work by economists Nancy Folbre and Jayoung Yoon (2008) of the Harmonized European Time Use Survey, which covers a diverse set of European countries in terms

of average incomes, education levels and childcare policies, indicates that whether there is a decline in unpaid work time depends on the type of work. Folbre and Yoon find that time spent on housework, collecting fuel and firewood, and as unpaid family workers declines with GDP. But, time spent on the care of family members, especially children, increases. Both the total unpaid time spent on childcare increases, and the share of childcare time as a proportion of total unpaid work time also increases. In keeping with the terminology of this section, Folbre and Yoon's study indicates that direct care work – that which involves direct emotional or physical contact with others – increases, while time spent in indirect care work – housework or cooking – declines.

Folbre and Yoon go on to discuss a number of aspects of economic development and structural change that are likely to underlie the results of this study. Fertility decline typically accompanies economic development, as well as increases in life expectancy. This changes the structure of dependents and the resultant demands on unpaid care, partly reflecting the shift from child quantity to quality discussed in the context of the demographic gift to growth. Smaller households and fewer extended family members living together means that households must be more self-reliant. At the same time, to the extent that development is accompanied by an expansion in social welfare supports for the elderly (e.g. pensions), the relative demands of children on unpaid care time grow. The expansion of wage employment makes it more difficult to combine unpaid direct care with paid work. And finally, increases in the opportunity cost of women's time may increase their bargaining power in the household, enabling women to bargain for a shift in their work time from indirect care like housework to direct care of children. The increased marketization of care, both domestically and internationally, also facilitates the fulfillment of these preferences.

8.3 Gender Inequality and the Macroeconomic Relevance of Care

In a paper for a recent UNDESA project on the equal sharing of responsibilities between women and men, Shahra Razavi and Silke Staab argue that care has yet to be seen as a truly macroeconomic issue (Razavi and Staab 2008). They contend that care issues only garner attention when care crises seem to threaten the smooth functioning of the economy, as for instance when fertility decline in the advanced industrialized countries threatens the financial viability of the social welfare system, or the HIV/AIDS crisis makes such tremendous demands on the care resources of developing countries. Still, the fact that crises of care have become a policy issue because of how they weaken the social relations of production has brought a key aspect of gender inequality – the sexual division of labor and responsibility for care – to the forefront in a new and promising manner. But Razavi and Staab's basic point still stands: although it is recognized that

care crises disproportionately affect women, maintaining the supply of care is still treated as a microeconomic or private issue, and there is often an unstated resistance to devising truly public supports for unpaid care work.

For instance, consider the research and policy discussions around the burden of care in the HIV/AIDS crisis in Sub-Saharan Africa. Studies in a number of countries show that women shoulder the vast majority of the increased care burden brought about by HIV/AIDS (Kes and Swaminathan 2006; Razavi 2005; UNAIDS 2008). In terms of time use, much of the albeit limited research focuses on the loss of women's productive time as caregiving responsibilities mount (see Kes and Swminathan (2006) for a review). These insights have led to policy discussions that focus on the unequal gender distribution of care, such as the UNDESA project on the equal sharing of responsibilities between women and men. But the limits that care responsibilities impose on women is not a new issue, and extends far beyond the unequal distribution of unpaid care work in households.

As early as the late 1980s, feminist economists and others argued that the economic models underlying the logic of structural adjustment presumed virtually unlimited supplies of unpaid labor, much of it from women and girls and to the detriment of their families and communities (Bakker 1994, Benería and Feldman 1992; Benería and Roldan 1987; Elson 1991, 1995; Gladwin 1991; Sen and Grown 1987; Sparr 1994). The implicit presumption was that women providing unpaid care in the household sector would be able to compensate for cuts in public services while also increasing their paid work in expanding export sectors. Evidence from the various waves of global economic crisis since the debt crisis of the early 1980s indicates that women and girls do in fact take on the majority of the social costs of crisis, with women and girls shouldering greater overall workloads as men's productive time declines (Elson 2009; Holmes, Jones and Marsden 2009; Knowles, Pernai and Racelis 1999). The social and economic consequences of these inequalities have contributed to efforts to better incorporate the "social" in structural adjustment policies, and to also be more careful about the sequencing and social content of economic reform in what is now commonly called a "post-Washington consensus." Still, even though some of the rhetoric of structural adjustment has changed, standard approaches to accounting for the social are often blind when it comes to the provisioning of care.

Social welfare and employment policies have long been characterized by what Diane Elson and Nilufer Cagatay call "male breadwinner bias," the assumption that the reproductive sector is linked with the productive sector through a full-time breadwinner without significant family responsibilities (Elson and Cagatay 2000). " 'Male breadwinner' bias constructs the ownership of rights to make claims on the state for social benefits (access to services, cash transfers) around a norm of full-time, life-long working-age participation in the market-based labor force." (Ibid.: 1355) The result is that standard models of social welfare benefits and delivery systematically afford women fewer entitlements because of their unpaid care work responsibilities. Whereas investments in education and health are seen as direct producers of human capital and therefore directly contributing to productive capacity, income supports for unpaid care work are often seen as wasteful welfare, and presume or reinforce unpaid care work as primarily women's responsibility (Razavi 2005).

For example, Mexico's Opportunidades is a means-tested program that gives poor mothers cash transfers for sending children to school, with girls getting a bigger stipend to counterbalance gender discrimination in education. To receive the stipend, mothers are required to meet a number of different often time-consuming conditions, including attending meetings and volunteering in the community (Razavi 2005). The program has been quite successful in raising school attendance and improving nutrition, but it has also raised women's workloads in ways that solidify the unpaid responsibilities of motherhood (Ibid.). Razavi (2005) cites South Africa's Old Age Pension as an example of a social welfare program that avoids stereotypes about unpaid care work while recognizing its value. South Africa's Old Age Pension system is also a means-tested program, but it provides income supports for elders (women at age 60 and men at age 65) regardless of their paid employment history, and has been an important way of supporting the many grandmothers caring for grandchildren orphaned by HIV/AIDS.

One way to draw these issues into the macroeconomic realm is to think in terms of the aggregate distribution of care responsibilities. There are different but complementary ways to get at this. Economist Nancy Folbre suggests a set of new indices aimed at measuring the gender distribution of care along lines similar to UNDP's GDI or GEM (Folbre 2006). The gender care spending parity index would measure private male spending on dependent care as a proportion of all private spending (male plus female), multiplied by two; a value of one would indicate gender equality in shouldering the private monetary costs of care. The gender direct care parity index would use the same formula only that it would reflect time rather than financial contributions to care. An overall care parity index would combine financial and time contributions, assigning a monetary value to unpaid care time. If we had good systematic, cross-country indices along the lines Folbre suggests, we could gain a better understanding of the role of the gender distribution of care in the macroeconomy, and the impact of economic development and crisis on that distribution.

In addition to accounting for the private distribution of care, it is also essential to account for the distribution between public and private. The work now being done on gender budgeting, where government revenue and expenditure is evaluated from a gender perspective, offers a good analytical framework and organizational model for evaluating public support for care (for examples, see Budlender and Hewitt 2003; UNIFEM 2002); more recent efforts seek to evaluate international aid programs from a gender-aware perspective as well (UNIFEM 2008). Paid care services in health, education and community services constitute a majority of government budgets in many countries (Sharp 2003). As noted above, when public spending for paid care services is cut, it is most often women and girls who pay the price. Infrastructure spending, and the extent to which it alleviates different types of unpaid work for women versus men, is another important area of analysis. But creating a set of standards for the systematic analysis of care, both paid and unpaid, in these and other development program contexts is yet to be achieved. Care issues are certainly a part of the gender and development policy discussions, but there is a difference between being referenced and being used as a regular indicator to assess policy and decision-making processes. A big part of this is simply lack of data and macroeconomic models. For instance, we know a lot more about the relationship between government spending and employment because these issues have been at the center of development discussions for decades. The work of UNRISD, UNIFEM and others is essential in moving our understanding of care and the macroeconomy forward, but much work remains to be done.

CHAPTER 9   **CONCLUDING REMARKS**

This report surveyed the gender and economic development literature, with particular emphasis on drawing out the gendered nature of micro/meso/macro linkages in economic relationships. In this section, we briefly review the issues covered from three vantage points: a summary overview of the main gender differences in economic development, a review of the key causal pathways of these differences discussed in the report, and some concluding remarks on the importance of promoting gender equality in economic development.

9.1 Gender Differences in Economic Development

The latter half of this report focused on four key policy areas in gender and economic development. The first two, on globalization and women's employment and the gendered terrain of central bank policy, emphasized how macroeconomic policies have gender-differentiated effects at the meso- and micro-levels. In both cases, labor market segregation by gender, and the unequal terms upon which women participate in labor markets, shaped how macroeconomic policy plays out at both the individual and community levels. Liberalization constrains the ability of states and communities to provide the types of social protections necessary for women to benefit from the empowerment effects of the increased employment that can accompany globalization. Gender-blind deflationary monetary policy not only dampens economic growth, but it does so in ways that exacts higher costs from women's employment than men's in developing countries, though

the choice of monetary policy instrument may attenuate this effect. The second two policy questions, the relationship between gender equality and economic growth and the macroeconomics of care, underscored how micro- and meso- relationships structure macroeconomic outcomes. In the case of gender equality and economic growth, discrimination against women in the social and economic arenas exacts quantifiable costs for economic growth, though gender-based wage inequality that does not detract from human capital development has been associated with higher rates of growth when it enhances global competitiveness. Considering care from a macroeconomic perspective illustrates how gendered social norms render the production of human capabilities invisible at the macroeconomic level, severely limiting the potential for economic analyses and policy to adequately address issues of human development and well-being. All four of these policy areas share a number of themes:

The gendered care gap. Regardless of the level of economic development, women around the world are still primarily responsible for the vast majority of household work and unpaid care. This sexual division of labor constrains women's abilities to participate in economic life, both in terms of practical time availability and the perpetuation of norms that devalue women's economic potential. These norms also give rise to economic models and policy that wrongly presume unlimited supplies of caring labor, with negative consequences for women and macroeconomic policy effectiveness.

Inequality in rights and resources. Women typically enter the economic arena at a disadvantage relative to men not just because of their work roles in the family, but also because of systematic marginalization from the types of rights and resources that are essential for economic participation and empowerment. Legal inequalities in *de jure* and *de facto* property rights and family law pose significant obstacles for many women in the developing world. And widespread discrimination against women in the allocation of resources, whether it be a family system that prioritizes the education of sons over daughters, or exclusion from markets for credit, land, or labor, limit women's economic participation in ways that perpetuate gender inequality.

Inequality at work. Partly as a result of the gender care gap, women are incorporated into labor markets on unequal terms relative to men, across all development paths (UNRISD 2010). Women have lower labor force participation rates than men; there is extensive gender segregation by occupation and industry, a type of segregation that tends to restrict women to the lowest-paid and otherwise less desirable sectors of the labor market; women earn less money than men, even when they engage in similar work; and women work fewer hours in the market than men, largely because of their household responsibilities (Ibid. 2010).

Inequality in economic decision-making. Women's interests and experiences are not well-represented in economic decision-making, whether it be at the microeconomic level of the family farm or household labor supply decisions, the meso-level of credit markets or development institutions, or the macro-level of monetary and fiscal policies. Though most research and policy interventions have focused on intra-household bargaining and its effect on household resource allocation and production decisions, leading to a pretty solid understanding of the microeconomic dynamics of gender and decision-making, much less is known about the effects of

women's absence in the public policy-making arena.

9.2 Causal Mechanisms

To understand the causal mechanisms of these gender differences in economic development, we refer back to the analytical micro-, meso- and macro-models presented in section 4. At the microeconomic level, gendered structures of constraint – the gender-specific norms, preferences, assets and rules that define what is both possible and desirable for women and men – combine with an individual's priorities and needs to determine provisioning capacity. Because collective households exhibit varying degrees of conflict and cooperation, intra-household bargaining, a process mediated by an individual's terms of household exit and their very ability to bargain (voice), determines the extent to which family decisions reflect the priorities and needs of particular household members. Gender, of course, is key to every component in this process, from the gendered norms and preferences that shape which options are considered possible, to the gendered property rights and family law that determine how women and men fare should they decide to leave the family.

These gendered dynamics are reflected and reconstituted in the meso- and macro-levels of the economy, both of which are "bearers of gender" in the sense of being structured by institutions and systems of advantage and disadvantage that themselves are gendered (Elson 1994). The macroeconomy is an emergent result of interactions between meso-level sectors and institutions, which are in turn built on the foundation of microeconomic relations – though the pathways run both ways. For instance, the structure of production in the domestic sector, which includes both households and communities, is where social reproduction, or the production of human capabilities via a combination of people and commodities, takes place. When the flow of income, goods and services, and the supply of time and natural assets are not enough to maintain social reproduction, human capabilities get depleted, which in turn will detract from macroeconomic growth, putting further pressure on the care economy. Labor market and education discrimination against women, a result of gender norms and stereotypes, manifests not only in lower rates of economic participation and incomes for women, but also as lower rates of economic growth.

The macro- and meso-levels also display their own characteristics, existing differently and independently of the micro-social relations that undergird them. For instance, gender bias within development institutions charged with creating and administering development programs is being addressed by a variety of gender-mainstreaming efforts, but these efforts are themselves hampered by a lack of understanding of the institutional (or meso-level) dynamics of that bias, as discussed in section 2.3. Economic models of the inflation-employment tradeoff used by central bank analysts are consistently gender-blind but not gender-neutral, with potentially deleterious effects on long-term economic growth, an effect that echoes the points made by Diane Elson and others about the short-sightedness of structural adjustment programs (Elson 1995).

9.3 On the Importance of Promoting Gender Equality

It is essential to promote gender equality as a goal of development on its own merits. Part of the reason is that economic growth itself does not ensure gender equality. For instance, evidence from India shows that increased agricultural growth has been accompanied by increasing male-female sex ratios and diminished well-being for the girls who do survive (UNRISD 2010: 107). In China, traditional son preference, the one-child family policy, and the lack of social security for the elderly have contributed to sex selective abortions and neglect for infant girls (Ibid.). Gender-based inequality in wages and time use persist in industrialized countries, and in the developing world, women are taking on an increasing share of informal work even where industrialization and growth have been robust. Integrating women into labor markets and the modern economy does not address some of the main sources of women's inequality, such as the gender division of care work. Growth must be accompanied by the types of structural and social changes that truly transform the socioeconomic relations of gender inequality. Changes in economic structure, such as infrastructural supports (e.g. transportation and sanitation) and social services that make it easier for women to combine their productive and reproductive roles, as well as the creation of high-quality employment opportunities that do not limit women to the lower reaches of the labor market, and changes in social relations such as the equal sharing of care responsibilities between women and men at the micro-, meso-, and macro-levels, must accompany growth to witness fundamental changes in gender inequality (DAW 2008; UNRISD 2010).

Taken from another perspective, there is the argument that gender equality has instrumental – and compelling – salutary effects on poverty and economic growth. However, that is not why gender equality should be prioritized. The point of economic development is not merely to raise growth rates or to speed up industrialization and modernization. The point of economic development is human development, as long emphasized by the UN and others. At best, economic growth is a somewhat vulgar proxy for human development. Gender equality is an essential part of achieving higher human development, and should thus be promoted as goal of development rather than simply a means to an end.

REFERENCES

Aghion, Philippe, Eve Caroli and Cecilia García-Penalosa. 1999. "Inequality and Economic Growth: The Perspective of the New Growth Theories." *Journal of Economic Literature* 37(4): 1615-1660.

Ahituv, Avner and Omer Moav. 2003. "Fertility Clubs and Economic Growth," in Theo S. Eicher and Stephen J. Turnovsky (eds.) *Inequality and Growth. Theory and Policy Implications.* Cambridge, MA: The MIT Press.

Alesina, Alberto and Dani Rodrik. 1994. "Distributive Politics and Economic Growth." *Quarterly Journal of Economics* 109(2): 465-490.

Algan, Yann and Pierre Cahuc. 2004. "Job Protection: The Macho Hypothesis." Society for Economic Dynamics, 2004 Meeting Papers No. 332, September.

Amsden, Alice H. 1989. *Asia's Next Giant: South Korea and Late Industrialization.* New York and Oxford: Oxford University Press.

Arriagada, Irma. 1994. "Changes in the Urban Female Labour Market." *CEPAL Review* 53: 92-110.

Aslanbeigui, Nahid and Gale Summerfield. 2000. "The Asian Crisis, Gender, and the International Financial Architecture." *Feminist Economics* 6(3): 81-103.

Azmat, Ghazala, Maia Güell and Alan Manning. 2006. "Gender Gaps in Unemployment Rates in OECD Countries." *Journal of Labor Economics* 24(1): 1-38.

Bacchetta, Marc, Ekkehard Ernst and Juana P. Bustamante. 2009. *Globalization and Informal Jobs in Developing Countries.* Geneva: World Trade Organization and International Labour Organization.

Bakker, Isabella (ed.) 1994. *The Strategic Silence: Gender and Economic Policy.* London: Zed Books.

Barnett, Katherine and Caren Grown. 2004. *Gender Impacts of Government Revenue Collection: The Case of Taxation.* London: Commonwealth Secretariat.

Barrientos, Armando. 2010. "Social Protection and Poverty." UNRISD Social Policy and Development Programme Paper No. 42.

Barrientos, Stephanie, Naila Kabeer and Naomi Hossain. 2004. *The gender dimensions of the globalization of production*, Working Paper No. 17 (Geneva, Policy Integration Department, ILO).

Bénabou, Roland. 2000. "Unequal Societies: Income Distribution and the Social Contract." *American Economic Review* 90(1): 96-129.

Benería, Lourdes. 2001a. "Introduction," in Lourdes Benería with Savitri Bisnath (eds.) *Gender and Development: Theoretical, Empirical and Practical Approaches.* Northampton, MA: Edward Elgar, pp. xi-xxi.

_____. 2001b. "Shifting the Risk: New Employment Patterns, Informalization, and Women's Work." *International Journal of Politics, Culture and Society* 15(1): 27-53.

Benía, Lourdes and Shelley Feldman (eds.) 1992. *Unequal Burden: Economic Crises, Persistent Poverty, and Women's Work.* Boulder, CO: Westview Press.

Benía, Lourdes and Martha Roldan. 1987. *The Crossroads of Class and Gender: Industrial Homework, Subcontracting, and Household Dynamics in Mexico City.* Chicago: University of Chicago Press.

Benía, Lourdes and Gita Sen. 1982. "Class and gender inequalities and women's role in economic development – theoretical and practical implications." *Feminist Studies* 8(1): 157-176.

Benía, Lourdes and Gita Sen. 1981. "Accumulation, reproduction, and women's role in economic development: Boserup revisited." *Signs* 7(2): 279-298.

Bergmann, Barbara. 1974. "Occupational Segregation, Wages and Profits When Employers Discriminate by Race or Sex." *Eastern Economic Journal* 1(2): 103-110.

Blackden, C. Mark and Chitra Bhanu. 1999. *Gender, Growth, and Poverty Reduction. Special Program of Assistance for Africa, 1998 Status Report on Poverty in Sub-Saharan Africa.* World Bank Technical Paper No. 428.

Blecker, Robert and Stephanie Seguino. 2002. "Macroeconomic Effects of Reducing Gender Wage Inequality in an Export-Oriented, Semi-industrialized Economy." *Review of Development Economics* 6(1): 103-119.

Bloom, David E. and Jeffrey G. Williamson. 1997. "Demographic Transitions and Economic Miracles in Emerging Asia." NBER Working Paper No. 6268.

Blumberg, Rae. 1991. "Income under female versus male control," in Rae Blumberg (ed.) *Gender, Family and Economy: The Triple Overlap.* Newbury Park, CA: Sage Press.

Braunstein, Elissa. 2008. "Making Policy Work for Women: Gender, Foreign Direct Investment, and Development," in Gunseli Berik, Yana van der Meulen Rodgers and Ann Zammit (eds.) *Social Justice and Gender Equality: Rethinking Development Strategies and Macroeconomic Policies,* London: Routledge.

_____. 2006. "Women's Work, Autonomy and Reproductive Health: The Role of Trade and Investment Liberalization," in Caren Grown, Elissa Braunstein and Anju Malhotra (eds.) *Trade Women's Health and Rights? Trade Liberalization and Reproductive Health in Developing Economies,* London: Zed Books.

Braunstein, Elissa and Gerald Epstein. 1999. "Creating international credit rules and the Multilateral Agreement on Investment: What are the alternatives?" in Jonathan Michie and John Grieve Smith (eds.) *Global Instability: The Political Economy of World Economic Governance.* London and New York: Routledge Press.

Braunstein Elissa and Nancy Folbre. 2001. "To honor and obey: Efficiency, inequality and patriarchal property rights." *Feminist Economics* 7(1): 25-44.

Braunstein, Elissa and James Heintz. 2008. "Gender Bias and Central Bank Policy: Employment and Inflation Reduction." *International Review of Applied Economics* 22(2): 173-186.

Braunstein, Elissa and Mark Brenner. 2007. "Foreign direct investment and wages in Urban China: The differences between women and men." *Feminist Economics* 13(3–4): 213–237.

Budlender, Debbie. 2008. "The Statistical Evidence on Care and Non-Care Work across Six Countries." Gender and Development Programme Paper No. 4, UNRISD.

Budlender, Debbie and Guy Hewitt. 2003. *Engendering Budgets: A Practitioners' Guide to Understanding and Implementing Gender-Responsive Budgets*. London: The Commonwealth Secretariat.

Buvinic Mayra and Andrew R. Morrison. 2008. "Introduction, Overview and Future Policy Agenda," in Mayra Buvinic, Andrew R. Morrison, A. Waafas Ofosu-Amaah and Mirja Sjöblom (eds.) *Equality for Women: Where Do We Stand on Millennium Development Goal 3?* Washington, D.C.: World Bank.

Çagatay, Nilüfer. 2001. *Trade, Gender and Poverty*. Background Paper commissioned as part of the Trade and Sustainable Development Project. New York: United Nations Development Programme.

Cagatay, Nilufer and Sule Ozler. 1995. "Feminization of the Labor Force: The Effects of Long-Term development and Structural Adjustment." *World Development* 23(11): 1883-94.

Carr, M., M. Alter Chen and J. Tate. 2000. "Globalization and home-based workers." *World Development* 6(3): 123-142.

Casale, Daniela 2003. "The rise in female labour force participation in South Africa: an analysis of household survey data, 1995-2001," Ph.D. dissertation, Division of Economics, University of KwaZulu-Natal.

Cerrutti, Marcela. 2000. "Economic Reform, Structural Adjustment and Female Labor Force Participation in Buenos Aires, Argentina." *World Development* 28(5): 879-891.

Chant, Sylvia. 2000. "From 'Woman-Blind' to 'Man-Kind': Should Men Have More Space in Gender and Development?" *IDS Bulletin* 31(2): 7-17.

Charmes, Jacques. 2006. "A Review of Empirical Evidence on Time use in Africa from UN-Sponsored Surveys," in C. Mark Blackden and Quentin Wodon (eds.) *Gender, Time Use, and Poverty in Sub-Saharan Africa. World* Bank Working Paper No. 73.

Chhachhi, Amrita. 2009. "Democratic Citizenship or Market-based Entitlements? A Gender Perspective on Social Protection in South Asia." International Institute for Social Studies Working Paper No. 486, The Hague, The Netherlands.

Clark, Robert L., Anne York and Richard Anker. 2003. "Cross-national Analysis of Women in the Labour Market," in Brigida Garcia, Richard Anker and Antonella Pinnelli (eds.) *Women in the labour market in changing economies: Demographic issues*. London: Oxford University Press, pp. 13-34.

Collier, Paul. 1994. "Gender aspects of labor allocation during structural adjustment: A theoretical framework and the Africa experience," in S. Horton, R. Kanbur and D. Mazumdar (eds.) *Labor Markets in an Era of Adjustment*, Vol. 1. Washington, D.C.: The World Bank.

Corner, Lorraine. 2009. "Gender Analysis of Fiscal Responses to the Economic Crisis in Asia." Presented at the UNRSID conference on the "Social and Political Dimensions of the Global Crisis: Implications for Developing Countries." Nov. 12-13, Geneva.

Deere, Carmen Diana and Magdalena Leon. 2001. *Empowering Women: Land and Property Rights in Latin America*. Pittsburgh: University of Pittsburgh Press.

Dijkstra, A. Geske. 2002. "Revisiting UNDP's GDI and GEM: Towards an alternative." *Social Indicators Research* 57(3): 301–338.

Division for the Advancement of Women (DAW). 2008. "The equal sharing of responsibilities between women and men, including caregiving in the context of HIV/AIDS." Report of the Expert Group Meeting, Division for the Advancement of Women, United Nations Department of Economic and Social Affairs, Geneva, Switzerland, October 6-9.

Dollar, David, Raymond Fisman and Roberta Gatti. 2001. "Are women really the "fairer" sex? Corruption and women in government." *Journal of Economic Behavior and Organization* 46: 423-429.

Dollar, David and Roberta Gatti. 1999. *Gender Inequality, Income, and Growth: Are Good Times Good for Women?* World Bank Policy Research Report Working Paper Series No. 1.

Doss, Cheryl. 2005. "The Effects of Intrahousehold Property Ownership on Expenditure Patterns in Ghana." *Journal of African Economies* 15: 149-80.

Duflo, Ester. 2005. "Gender Equality in Development." Unpublished ms., Massachusetts Institute of Technology.

Dwyer, Daisy and Judith Bruce. 1988. *A home divided: Women and income in the Third World.* Stanford, CA: Stanford University Press.

Economic Commission for Latin America and the Caribbean (ECLAC). 2010. *Achieving the Millennium Development Goals With Equality in Latin America and the Caribbean: Progress and Challenges.* Santiago, Chile: United Nations.

Elson, Diane. 2009. "Social Reproduction in the Global Crisis." Presentation notes for UNRISD conference on Social and Political Dimensions of the Global Crisis, Geneva, Nov. 12-13.

_____. 2005. "Unpaid Work, the Millennium Development Goals, and Capital Accumulation, Notes for a presentation." Conference on Unpaid Work and the Economy: Gender, Poverty, and the Millennium Development Goals, Levy Economics Institute, October 1-3.

_____. 1999. "Theories of Development," in Janice Peterson and Margaret Lewis (eds.) *The Elgar Companion to Feminist Economics.* Cheltenham: Edward Elgar, 95-107.

_____. 1998. "The Economic, the Political and the Domestic: Businesses, States and Households in the Organisation of Production." *New Political Economy* 3(2): 189-208.

_____. 1997. "Economic Paradigms and Their Implications for Models of Development: The Case of Human Development," in Roy Culpeper, Albert Berry and Frances Stewart (eds.) *Global Governance and Development Fifty Years after Bretton Woods: Essays in Honour of Gerald K Helleiner.* London: Palgrave Macmillan.

_____. 1996. "Appraising recent developments in the world market for nimble fingers," in Amrita Chhachhi and Renée Pittin (eds.), *Confronting State, Capital and Patriarchy: Women' Organizing in the Process of Industrialization.* St. Martin's Press: New York.

_____. 1995. "Gender Awareness in Modeling Structural Adjustment." *World Development* 23(11): 1851-1868.

_____. 1994. "Micro, Meso, Macro: Gender and Economic Analysis in the Context of Policy Reform," in Isabella Bakker (ed.) *The Strategic Silence: Gender and Economic Policy*. London: Zed Books.

_____. 1991. "Male bias in macro-economics: the case of structural adjustment," in Diane Elson (ed.) *Male Bias in the Development Process*. Manchester and New York: Manchester University Press.

Elson, Diane and Nilufer Cagatay. 2000. "The Social Content of Macroeconomic Policies." *World Development* 28(7): 1347-1364.

Elson, Diane and Ruth Pearson. 1981. "Nimble fingers make cheap workers: An analysis of women's employment in third world export manufacturing,"*Feminist Review* 7:87-107.

Epstein, Gerald. 2003. "Alternative to Inflation Targeting Monetary Policy for Stable and Egalitarian Growth: A Brief Research Summary." PERI Working Paper No. 62.

_____. 2000. "Myth, Mendacity and Mischief in the Theory and Practice of Central Banking." Manuscript, University of Massachusetts Amherst.

Epstein, Gerald and Erinc Yeldan (eds.) 2009. *Beyond Inflation Targeting: Assessing the Impacts and Policy Alternatives*. Cheltenham, UK and Northampton, MA: Edward Elgar.

Esteve-Volart, Berta. 2004. "Gender Discrimination and Growth: Theory and Evidence from India." Unpublished ms., London School of Economics and Political Science.

_____.2000. "Sex Discrimination and Growth." International Monetary Fund Working Paper.

Feenstra, Robert and Gordon Hanson. 1997. " Foreign Direct Investment and Relative Wages: Evidence from Mexico's Maquiladoras." *Journal of International Economics* 42: 371-393.

Folbre, Nancy. 2006. "Measuring Care: Gender, Empowerment, and the Care Economy." *Journal of Human Development* 7(2): 183-199.

_____. 1997. "Gender coalitions: Extrafamily influences on intrafamily inequality," in L. Haddad, J. Hoddinott, and H. Alderman (eds.) *Intrahousehold Resource Allocation in Developing Countries. Models, Methods, and Policy*. Baltimore: The Johns Hopkins University Press.

_____. 1994. *Who Pays for the Kids? Gender and the Structures of Constraint*. London and New York: Routledge.

_____. 1991. "Women on their own: Global patterns of female headship," in R. Gallin and A. Ferguson (eds.) *The Women and International Development Annual Volume 2*. Boulder: Westview Press.

_____. 1986. "Hearts and Spades: Paradigms of Household Economics." *World Development* 14(2): 245-55.

Folbre, Nancy and Jayoung Yoon. 2008. "Economic Development and Time Devoted to Direct Unpaid Care Activities: An Analysis of the Harmonized European Time Use Survey (HETUS)." Background paper commissioned for the UNRISD Flagship Report on Poverty.

Fontana, Giuseppe and Palacio-Vera, Alfonso. 2004. "Is long-run price stability and short-run output stabilization all that monetary policy can do?" Mimeo. University of Leeds and Universidad Complutense de Madrid.

Fontana, Marzia. 2009. "The Gender Effects of Trade Liberalization in Developing Countries: A Review of the Literature," in M. Bussolo and R. De Hoyos (eds.) *Gender Aspects of the Trade and Poverty Nexus: A Micro-Macro Approach*. Basingstoke: Palgrave Macmillan.

Food and Agriculture Organization of the United Nations (FAO). 2009. "Forests." http://www.fao.org/gender/gender-home/gender-programme/gender-forests/en/, accessed Dec. 21, 2009.

Forsythe, Nancy, Roberto Patricio Korzeniewicz and Valerie Durrant. 2000. "Gender Inequalities and Economic Growth: A Longitudinal Evaluation." *Economic Development and Cultural Change* 48(3): 573-617.

Fussell, Elizabeth. 2000. "Making labor flexible: The recomposition of Tijuana's Maquiladora female labor force." *Feminist Economics* 6(3): 59-79.

Galor, Oded and David N. Weil. 1996. "The Gender Gap, Fertility and Growth." *The American Economic Review* 86(3): 374-387.

Ghosh, Jayati. 2007. "Informalization, migration and women: Recent trends in Asia," in Debdas Banerjee and Michael Goldfield (eds.) *Labour, globalization and the state: Workers, women and migrants confront neoliberalism*. London: Routledge.

Gladwin, Christina (ed.) 1991. *Structural Adjustment and African Women Farmers*. Gainesville: University of Florida Press.

Goldschmidt-Clermont, Luisella. 1993. "Monetary Valuation of Non-market Productive Time. Methodological Considerations." *Review of Income and Wealth* 39(4): 419-433.

Greenhalgh, Susan. 1985. "Sexual Stratification: The Other Side of 'Growth with Equity' in East Asia." *Population and Development Review* 11(2): 265-314.

Grown Caren. 2008a. "Gender and Development," in William Darity, Jr. (ed.) *International Encyclopedia of the Social Sciences, 2nd ed.* Detroit: Macmillan Reference.

_____. 2008b. "Indicators and Indexes of Gender Inequality: What Do They Measure and What Do They Miss?" in Mayra Buvinic, Andrew R. Morrison, A. Waafas Ofosu-Amaah and Mirja Sjöblom (eds.) *Equality for Women: Where Do We Stand on Millennium Development Goal 3?* Washington, D.C.: World Bank.

Grown, Caren, Geeta Rao Gupta, Aslihan Kes and the UN Millennium Project Task Force on Education and Gender Equality. 2005. *Taking action: Achieving gender equality and empowering women*. London: Earthscan.

Grown, Caren and Imraan Valodia (eds.) 2010. *Taxation and Gender Equity. A Comparative Analysis of Direct and Indirect Taxes in Developing and Developed Countries*. London: Routledge.

Hanson, Gordon and Ann Harrison. 1999. "Trade, Technology, and Wage Inequality." *Industrial and Labor Relations Review* 52: 271-88.

Hausmann, Ricardo, Laura D. Tyson, and Saadia Zahidi. 2009. *The Global Gender Gap Index Report 2009*. Geneva: World Economic Forum.

Hill, M. Anne and Elizabeth M. King. 1995. "Women's education and economic well-being." *Feminist Economics*, Vol. 1, No. 2, pp. 21-46.

Hirway, Indira and Seeta Prabhu. 2009. "Restructuring Development during Global Financial Crisis." Presented at the UNRSID conference on the "Social and Political Dimensions of the Global Crisis: Implications for Developing Countries." Nov. 12-13, Geneva.

Hoddinott, John, Harold Alderman, and Lawrence Haddad, eds. 1998. *Intrahousehold Resource Allocation in Developing Countries: Methods, Models and Policy.* Baltimore: Johns Hopkins University Press.

Holmes, Rebecca, Nicola Jones and Hannah Marsden. 2009. "Gender vulnerabilities, food price shocks and social protection responses." ODI Background note, August.

Howes, Candace and Ajit Singh. 1995. "Long-term trends in the World Economy: The Gender Dimension." *World Development* 23(11): 1895-1912.

Hsiung, Ping-Chun. 1996. *Living Rooms as Factories: Class, Gender, and the Satellite Factory System in Taiwan.* Philadelphia: Temple University Press.

International Labour Organization (ILO). 2009. *Global Employment Trends for Women March 2009.* Geneva: International Labour Office.

International Monetary Fund (IMF). 2010. *World Economic Outlook Update,* January 26. Downloaded on Feb. 10, 2010, http://www.imf.org/external/pubs/ft/weo/2010/update/01/index.htm.

Ironmonger, Duncan. 1996. "Counting Outputs, Capital Inputs and Caring Labor: Estimating Gross Household Product." *Feminist Economics* 2(3): 37-64.

Jackson, Cecile, and Ruth Pearson (eds.) 1998. *Feminist Visions of Development: Gender Analysis and Policy.* London: Routledge.

Joekes, Susan. 1999. "A gender-analytical perspective on trade and sustainable development," *Trade, Sustainable Development and Gender.* New York and Geneva: UNCTAD.

Joireman, S.F. 2008. "The Mystery of Capital Formation in Sub-Saharan Africa: Women, Property Rights and Customary Law." *World Development* 36(7): 1233-1246.

Katz, Elizabeth. 1997. "The intra-household economics of voice and exit," *Feminist Economics* 3(3): 25-46.

Kabeer, Naila. 2000. *The Power to Choose: Bangladeshi Women and Labour Market Decisions in London and Dhaka.* London and New York: Verso.

_____. 1999. "Resources, agency, achievements: Reflections on the measurement of women's empowerment." *Development and Change.* 30: 435-434.

_____. 1994. *Reversed Realities: Gender Hierarchies in Development Thought.* London: Verso.

Kes, Aslihan and Hema Swaminathan. 2006. "Gender and Time Poverty in Sub-Saharan Africa," in C. Mark Blackden and Quentin Wodon (eds.) *Gender, Time Use, and Poverty in Sub-Saharan Africa.* World Bank Working Paper No. 73.

Kishor, S. 1997. "Empowerment of women in Egypt and links to the survival and health of the infants," Paper presented at the Seminar on Female Empowerment and Demographic Processes, Lund, 20-24 April.

Klasen, Stephan. 2006. "UNDP's Gender-Related Measures: Some Conceptual Problems and Possible Solutions." *Journal of Human Development* 7(2): 243-74.

_____. 2005. "Pro Poor Growth and Gender: What can we learn from the literature and the OPPG case studies?" Discussion Paper to the Operationalizing Pro-Poor Growth (OPPG) Working Group of AFD, DFID, BMZ and the World Bank.

_____. 2002. "Low Schooling for Girls, Slower Growth for All? Cross-Country Evidence on the Effect of Gender Inequality in Education on Economic Development." *The World Bank Economic Review* 16(3): 345-373.

_____. 1999. *Does Gender Inequality Reduce Growth and Development? Evidence from Cross-Country Regressions*. World Bank Policy Research Report on Gender and Development, Working Paper Series No. 7, World Bank, Washington, D.C.

Klasen, Stephen and Francesca Lamanna. 2009. "The Impact of Gender Inequality in Education and Employment on Economic Growth: New Evidence for a Panel of Countries." *Feminist Economics* 15(3): 91-132.

Knowles, James, Ernesto Pernia and Mary Racelis. 1999. "Social Consequences of the Financial Crisis in Asia." Economic Staff Paper No. 60, Asian Development Bank.

Knowles, Stephen, Paula K. Lorgelly, and P. Dorian Owen. 2002. "Are educational gender gaps a brake on economic development? Some cross-country empirical evidence." *Oxford Economic Papers* 54: 118-149.

Lim, Linda. 1990. "Women's work in export factories: The politics of a cause," in Irene Tinker (ed.) *Persistent Inequalities: Women and World Development*. Oxford: Oxford University Press.

Lagerlöf, Nils-Peter. 2003. "Gender Equality and Long-run Growth." *Journal of Economic Growth* 8(4): 403-426.

Lundberg, Shelly J., Robert A. Pollak and Terence J. Wales. 1997. "Do Husbands and Wives Pool Their Resources? Evidence from the United Kingdom Child Benefit." *The Journal of Human Resources* 32(3): 463-480.

Milberg, William. 1998. "Technological change, social policy and international competitiveness." Working paper on Globalization, Labor Markets and Social Policy, New School for Social Research, New York.

Morrison, Andrew R., Shwetlena Sabarwal and Mirja Sjöblom. 2009. "The State of World Progress, 1990-2007," in Mayra Buvinic, Andrew R. Morrison, A. Waafas Ofosu-Amaah and Mirja Sjöblom (eds.) *Equality for Women: Where Do We Stand on Millennium Development Goal 3?* Washington, D.C.: World Bank.

Moser, Caroline O.N. 1993. Gender Planning and Development: Theory, Practice and Training. New York: Routledge.

Moser, Caroline and Annalise Moser. 2005. "Gender mainstreaming since Beijing: A review of success and limitations in international institutions, Fenella Porter and Caroline Sweetman (eds.) *Gender and Development: Mainstreaming: A critical review*. Oxford, U.K.: Oxfam Publishing, pp. 11-22.

Murthi, Mamta, Anne-Catherine Guio and Jean Dreze. 1995. "Mortality, Fertility, and Gender Bias in India: A District-Level Analysis." *Population and Development Review* 21(4): 745-782.

Palmer, Ingrid. 1992. "Gender equity and economic efficiency in adjustment models," in H. Afshar and C. Dennis (eds.) *Women and Adjustment Policies in the Third World*. London: Macmillan.

Patnaik, Utsa. 2003. "Global Capitalism, Deflation and Agrarian Crisis in Developing Countries." United Nations Research Institute for Social Development, Social Policy and Development Programme Paper Number 15, October.

Pearson, Ruth. 2004. "Women, work and empowerment in a global era." *IDS Bulletin* 35(4): 117-120.

Permanyer, Iñaki. 2010. "The Measurement of Multidimensional Gender Inequality: Continuing the Debate." *Social Indicators Research* 95(2): 181-198.

Perotti, Roberto. 1996. "Growth, Income Distribution, and Democracy: What the Data Say." *Journal of Economic Growth* 1(2): 149-187.

Persson, Torsten and Guido Tabellini. 1994. "Is Inequality Harmful for Growth?" *American Economic Review* 84(3): 600-621.

Pyatt, Graham. 1993. "Beyond the production boundary." Revision of a paper prepared for the Human Development Report Office, UNDP, as a basis for discussion.

Quisumbing, Agnes R. 2003. "What Have We Learned from Research on Intrahousehold Allocation?" In *Household Decisions, Gender and Development: A Synthesis of Recent Research*, edited by Agnes R. Quisumbing. Washington, D.C.: International Food Policy Research Institute.

Quisumbing, Agnes, Jonna Esutdillo and Keijiro Otsuka. 2004. *Land and Schooling: Transferring Wealth Across Generations*. Baltimore, MD: Johns Hopkins University Press.

Rao, Mohan. 1999. "Globalization and the fiscal autonomy of the state." Background paper for the *Human Development Report 1999*, New York: UNDP.

Rathgeber, Eva. 1990. "WID, WAD, GAD: Trends in Research and Practice." *The Journal of Developing Areas* 24(4): 489-502.

Razavi, Shahra. 2005. "The Relevance of Women's Unpaid Work to Social Policy in Developing Countries." Prepared for the Global conference on Unpaid Work and the Economy: Gender, Poverty and the Millennium Development Goals, Oct. 1-3, Bard College, New York.

Razavi, Shahra and Shireen Hassim (eds.) 2006. *Gender and Social Policy in a Global Context: Uncovering the Gendered Structure of "the Social."* New York: Palgrave MacMillan for UNRISD.

Razavi, Shahra and Carol Miller. 1995. "From WID to GAD: Conceptual Shifts in the Women and Development Discourse." United Nations Research Institute for Social Development, Occasional Paper 1, Geneva, Switzerland.

Razavi, Shahra and Silke Staab. 2008. "The Social and Political Economy of Care: Contesting Gender and Class Inequalities." Prepared for the Expert Group Meeting on "Equal sharing of responsibilities between women and men, including care-giving in the context of HIV/AIDS," Oct. 6-9, Geneva.

Rodrik, Dani. 1997. *Has Globalization Gone Too Far?* Washington, D.C.: Institute for International Economics.

Rodrik, Dani and Mark R. Rosenzweig. 2009. "Introduction: Linking Development Policy with Development Research," in Dani Rodrik and Mark R. Rosenzweig (eds.) Handbook of Development Economics, Vol. 5. North-Holland.

Rodrik, Dani, Arvind Subramanian and Francesco Trebbi. 2004. "Institutions Rule: The Primacy of Institutions over Geography and Integration in Economic Development." *Journal of Economic Growth* 9: 131-2004.

Roemer, John E. 2006. "The 2006 world development report: Equity and development." *Journal of Economic Inequality* 4: 233-244.

Saito, Katrine, Hailu Mekonnen, and Daphne Spurling. 1994. "Raising the productivity of women farmers in Sub-Saharan Africa." World Bank Discussion Papers, Africa Technical Department Series No. 230.

Schultz, T. Paul. 2005. "Does the Liberalization of Trade Advance Gender Equality in Schooling and Health?." Yale University Economic Growth Center Working Paper. 44 pages. *EconLit*, EBSCO*host* (accessed April 12, 2010).

_____. 2001. "Why Governments Should Investment More to Educate Girls." Unpublished ms., Yale University.

Seguino, Stephanie. 2008. "Gender, Distribution, and Balance of Payments Constrained Growth in Developing Countries." Unpublished ms., University of Vermont.

_____. 2003. "Why are Women in the Caribbean So Much More Likely Than Men to be Unemployed?" *Social and Economic Studies* 52(4): 83-120.

_____. 2000a. "Accounting for Gender in Asian Economic Growth." *Feminist Economics* 6(3): 27-58.

_____. 2000b. "The effects of structural change and economic liberalization on gender wage differentials in South Korea and Taiwan." *Cambridge Journal of Economics* 24(4): 437-459.

_____. 2000c. "Gender Inequality and Economic Growth: A Cross-Country Analysis." *World Development* 28(7): 1211-1230.

Seguino, Stephanie and Caren Grown. 2006. "Gender Equity and Globalization: Macroeconomic Policy for Developing Countries." *Journal of International Development* 18:1081-1114.

Sen, Amartya. 1984. *Resources, Values and Development*. London: Blackwell.

Sen, Gita and Caren Grown. 1987. *Development, Crises and Alternative Visions: Third World Women's Perspectives*. New York: Monthly Review Press.

Sharp, Rhonda. 2003. *Budgeting for equity: Gender budget initiatives within a framework of performance oriented budgeting*. New York: UNIFEM.

Social Watch. 2010. *Social Watch Gender Equity Index 2009*. Downloaded from http://www.socialwatch.org/node/11561 on March 29, 2010.

Solow, Robert M. 1956. "A Contribution to the Theory of Economic Growth." *The Quarterly Journal of Economics* 70(1): 65-94.

Sparr, Pam (ed.) 1994. *Mortgaging Women's Lives: Feminist Critiques of Structural Adjustment*. London: Zed Books for the United Nations.

Standing, Guy. 1999. "Global Feminization Through Flexible Labor: A Theme Revisited." *World Development* 27(3): 583-602.

_____. 1989. "Global Feminization through Flexible Labor." *World Development* 17(7): 1077-1095.

Standing, Hilary. 2007. "Gender, myth and fable: the perils of mainstreaming in sector bureaucracies,". in Andrea Cornwall, Elizabeth Harrison, and Ann Whitehead (eds.) *Feminisms in Development: Contradictions, Contestations & Challenges*. London & New York: Zed Press.

Swamy, Anand, Stephen Knack, Young Lee, and Omar Azfar. 2003. "Gender and Corruption," in Stephen Knack (ed.) *Democracy, Governance and Growth*. Ann Arbor, MI: University of Michigan Press.

Thomas, Duncan. 1997. "Incomes, Expenditures, and Health Outcomes: Evidence on Intrahousehold Resource Allocation," in L. Haddad, J. Hoddinott and H. Alderman (eds.) *Intrahousehold Resource Allocation in Developing Countries: Models, Methods and Policy*. Baltimore and London: Johns Hopkins University Press.

_____. 1990. "Intra-Household Resource Allocation. An Inferential Approach." *Journal of Human Resources* 25(4): 635-64.

Todaro, Michael P. and Stephen C. Smith. 2006. *Economic Development*. Ninth Edition. Boston: Pearson.

Tzannatos, Zafiris. 2009. "Monitoring Progress in Gender Equality in the Labor Market," in Mayra Buvinic, Andrew R. Morrison, A. Waafas Ofosu-Amaah and Mirja Sjöblom (eds.) *Equality for Women: Where Do We Stand on Millennium Development Goal 3?* Washington, D.C.: World Bank.

_____. 1999. "Women and Labor Market Changes in the Global Economy: Growth Helps, Inequalities Hurt and Public Policy Matters." *World Development* 27(3): 551-569.

Udry, Christopher. 1996. "Gender, Agricultural Production and the Theory of the Household." *The Journal of Political Economy* 104(5): 1010-1016.

Udry, Christopher, John Hoddinott, Harold Alderman, and Lawrence Haddad. 1995. "Gender differentials in farm productivity: Implications for household efficiency and agricultural policy." *Food Policy* 20(5): 407-423.

UNAIDS. 2008. "Caregiving in the context of HIV/AIDS." Prepared for the Expert Group Meeting on "Equal sharing of responsibilities between women and men, including care-giving in the context of HIV/AIDS," Oct. 6-9, Geneva.

United Nations (UN). 2009. *The Millennium Development Goals Report*. New York: United Nations.

_____. 2008. "Official list of MDG indicators," downloaded from http://mdgs.un.org/unsd/mdg/Host.aspx?Content=Indicators/OfficialList.htm, March 3, 2010.

_____. 2007. *Human Development Report 2007/2008*. New York: United Nations Development Programme.

_____. 1999. *World Survey on the Role of Women in Development. Globalization, Gender and Work*. New York: United Nations.

_____. 1997. "Report of the Economic and Social Council for 1997," A/52/3, 18 September.

_____. 1995. *Human Development Report 1995: The Revolution for Gender Equality.* New York: United Nations Development Programme.

United Nations Department of Economic and Social Affairs (UNDESA). 2004. *Guide to Producing Statistics on Time Use: Measuring Paid and Unpaid Work.* United Nations Publication ST/ESA/STAT/SER.F/93.

_____, Division for the Advancement of Women. 2009. *2009 World Survey on the Role of Women in Development: Women's Control over Economic Resources and Access to Financial Resources, including Microfinance.* New York: United Nations.

United Nations Development Fund for Women (UNIFEM). 2008. UNIFEM's Work in Support of Gender-Responsive Budgeting. Downloaded from http://www.gender-budgets.org/index.php?option=com_joomdoc&view=docman&gid=179&task=cat_view&Itemid=587 on April 26, 2010.

_____. 2005. "Unpaid Work and the Economy. UNIFEM and Time Use Studies." http://www.unifem.org/materials/fact_sheets.php?StoryID=378, downloaded on Feb. 6, 2010.

_____. 2002. *Gender Budget Initiatives: Strategies, Concepts and Experiences.* New York: UNIFEM.

United Nations Development Programme (UNDP). 2009. *Human Development Report 2009.* New York: Palgrave MacMillan for UNDP.

_____. 2008. *Innovative Approaches to Promoting Women's Economic Empowerment.* New York: UNDP.

United Nations Economic Commission for Africa (UNECA). 2009. *African Women's Report 2009: Measuring Gender Inequality in Africa: Experiences and Lessons from the African Gender and Development Index.* Addis Ababa, Ethiopia: UNECA.

United Nations Economic and Social Commission for Asia and the Pacific (UN-ESCAP). 2007. *Economic and Social Survey of Asia and the Pacific 2007: Surging Ahead in Uncertain Times.* Thailand: United Nations.

United Nations Research Institute for Social Development (UNRISD). 2010. *Combating Poverty and Inequality: Structural Change, Social Policy and Politics.* Geneva: UNRISD.

United Nations Research Institute for Social Development (UNRISD). 2005. *Gender Equality: Striving for Justice in an Unequal World.* Geneva: UNRISD.

World Bank. 2006. "Gender Equality as Smart Economics: A World Bank Group Gender Action Plan (Fiscal Years 2007-10). Downloaded from: www.worldbank.org, Accessed 12/7/09

_____. 2005. *World Development Report 2006: Equity and Development.* Washington, D.C. and New York: World Bank and Oxford University Press.

_____. 2001. *Engendering Development Through Equality in Rights, Resources, and Voice.* New York: Oxford University Press.

World Trade Organization (WTO). 2009. *International Trade Statistics 2009.* Geneva: WTO.

Young, Alwyn. 1995. "The Tyranny of Numbers: Confronting the Statistical Realities of the East Asian Growth Experience." *The Quarterly Journal of Economics* 110(3): 641-680.

APPENDIX A

Regional Groupings for Figures 8 & 9

Regional averages weighted by population. For all regions, only countries with data for HDI, GDI and GEM were used for regional averages with the exception of South Asia, where the full sample was used to figure HDI and GDI, but a much more limited one to figure GEM. Countries in red are not in regional averages due to lack of data.

Developed & EU (non-CIS)	Central & Eastern Europe & Commonwealth Independent States	East Asia & Pacific
Norway	Kazakhstan	Singapore
Australia	Slovenia	Hong Kong, China (SAR)
Iceland	Czech Republic	Korea (Republic of)
Canada	Estonia	Brunei Darussalam
Ireland	Poland	Malaysia
Netherlands	Slovakia	Thailand
Sweden	Hungary	China
France	Croatia	Samoa
Switzerland	Lithuania	Tonga
Japan	Latvia	Philippines
Finland	Bulgaria	Fiji
United States	Romania	Indonesia
Austria	Montenegro	Mongolia
Spain	Serbia	Viet Nam
Denmark	Belarus	Vanuatu
Belgium	Albania	Solomon Islands
Italy	Russian Federation	Lao People's Democratic Republic
New Zealand	The former Yugoslav Republic of Macedonia	Cambodia
United Kingdom	Bosnia and Herzegovina	Myanmar
Germany	Armenia	Papua New Guinea
Greece	Ukraine	Timor-Leste
Israel	Azerbaijan	Taiwan
Cyprus	Georgia	
Portugal	Turkmenistan	
Malta	Moldova	
Turkey	Uzbekistan	
	Kyrgyzstan	
	Tajikistan	

South Asia

Maldives

Iran (Islamic Republic of)

Sri Lanka

Bhutan

India

Pakistan

Bangladesh

Nepal

Afghanistan

Arab States

Kuwait

Qatar

United Arab Emirates

Bahrain

Libyan Arab Jamahiriya

Oman

Saudi Arabia

Lebanon

Jordan

Tunisia

Algeria

Syrian Arab Republic

Egypt

Morocco

Yemen

Sudan

Djibouti

Latin America & the Caribbean

Barbados

Chile

Antigua and Barbuda

Argentina

Uruguay

Cuba

Bahamas

Mexico

Costa Rica

Venezuela (Bolivarian Republic of)

Panama

Saint Kitts and Nevis

Trinidad and Tobago

Dominica

Grenada

Brazil

Colombia

Peru

Ecuador

Dominican Republic

Saint Vincent and the Grenadines

Belize

Suriname

Jamaica

Paraguay

El Salvador

Honduras

Bolivia

Guyana

Guatemala

Nicaragua

Haiti

Sub-Saharan Africa

Mauritius

Gabon

Equatorial Guinea

Cape Verde

Botswana

Namibia

South Africa

Sao Tome and Principe

Congo

Comoros

Swaziland

Angola

Madagascar

Kenya

Tanzania (United Republic of)

Ghana

Cameroon

Mauritania

Lesotho

Uganda

Nigeria

Togo

Malawi

Benin

Niger

Côte d'Ivoire

Zambia

Eritrea

Senegal

Rwanda

Gambia

Liberia

Guinea

Ethiopia

Mozambique

Guinea-Bissau

Burundi

Chad

Congo (Democratic Republic of the)

Burkina Faso

Mali

Central African Republic

Sierra Leone